To Sidney

June 14, 1930.

from

Mr. and Mrs. Noble

and Ceg.

BOOKS BY THE SAME AUTHOR

VILLAS OF FLORENCE AND TUSCANY
LITTLE KNOWN ENGLAND
MANOR HOUSES AND HISTORIC HOMES
  OF LONG ISLAND AND STATEN ISLAND
THE MANORS AND HISTORIC HOMES OF
  THE HUDSON VALLEY
THE ARCHITECTURE OF COLONIAL AMERICA

*By Harold Donaldson Eberlein, Abbot McClure
  and Edward Stratton Holloway*

THE PRACTICAL BOOK OF INTERIOR DECORATION

By Harold Donaldson Eberlein and Abbot McClure

THE PRACTICAL BOOK OF PERIOD FURNITURE
THE PRACTICAL BOOK OF AMERICAN ANTIQUES

*By Harold Donaldson Eberlein and
  Roger Wearne Ramsdell*

THE PRACTICAL BOOK OF CHINAWARE
THE PRACTICAL BOOK OF ITALIAN, SPANISH
  AND PORTUGUESE FURNITURE
SMALL MANOR HOUSES AND FARMSTEADS
  IN FRANCE

*By Harold Donaldson Eberlein and
  A. E. Richardson*

THE ENGLISH INN PAST AND PRESENT
THE SMALLER ENGLISH HOUSE OF THE LATER
  RENAISSANCE—1660-1830

The Old Bridge
Ponte San Giovanni

DOWN THE TIBER AND UP TO ROME

BY
HAROLD DONALDSON EBERLEIN
GEOFFREY J. MARKS
FRANK A. WALLIS

WITH FRONTISPIECE
IN COLOUR
AND 12 ILLUSTRATIONS
FROM DRAWINGS BY
FRANK A. WALLIS

PHILADELPHIA & LONDON
J. B. LIPPINCOTT COMPANY
MCMXXX

TO ITALY AND THE PEOPLE OF ITALY
IN WARM APPRECIATION OF
MANY KINDNESSES RECEIVED

FOREWORD

TO SEE any country, or any part of a country, from its natural waterways is to have its inmost character revealed without reservations, and in a fashion not so possible through any other means of approach.

We have long maintained that you must see a country by road in order really to know it, and we believe that our contention on this score is fully warranted. To see it from its waterways when, and so far as, that may be possible, is the only further perfection of travel we can suggest.

To pursue the course of the Tiber from source to mouth, and to make by canoe as much of that journey as physical conditions would permit, had long been a cherished ambition. Now that we have at last realised that ambition, and have traversed the stream in our *canotto di gomma* from Ponte San Giovanni to Rome, we are convinced that our fondest expectations were fully justified. The journey at times was troublesome and laborious, but we feel amply repaid for all our exertions. Looking back, we would not have the expedition in any respect otherwise than it was.

To those who wish to see a little-known part of Italy, fascinating for its natural beauty, rich in varied historical associations, endowed with its due share of the treasures of art and architecture, and affording most agreeable personal contacts, we can heartily recommend an expedition over the same ground. If the reader is not inclined to emulate the ardours of uncertain navigation, with a very few modifications it is perfectly feasible to traverse much the same territory by road. We found the advantages of our own method to be the enjoyment of the fresh and ever-changing river views. Views from the road will often be views from the back, as it were; views from the river are views from in front. The river outlook, too, has frequently a certain spaciousness not found ashore. Likewise, by road there will inevitably be sundry retracings of the way and the intermediate journeyings will sometimes be longer. Nevertheless the trip is heartily to be commended.

To some, *Down the Tiber and Up to Rome* may seem a title that carries a measure of physical contradiction. "How," say they, "can you go both *down* and *up* at the same time?" The answer is that you always go *up* to Rome, no matter where you may be starting from. You go *up* to Rome, just as the Jews of old always went *up* to Jerusalem, regardless of whether they were approaching it from north, south, east or west. You go *up* to Rome, even from London, for Rome is the senior city and takes precedence— at least, Rome is the source of our modern civilisation, and Rome was the fountain-head of authority during all those centuries when England was a part of the Roman Empire. Therefore, while from everywhere else we Anglo-Saxons may go *up* to London as the virtual centre of our universe, to Rome alone we go *up* from London, in obedience to time-honoured tradition and in dutiful conformity with the Classic proprieties firmly implanted in us by our schoolmasters in the tender years of our incipient Latinity. Rome is so much, and means so much, that we still regard a pilgrimage thither as a going up to the goal of desire.

HAROLD DONALDSON EBERLEIN
GEOFFREY J. MARKS
FRANK A. WALLIS

BROADWAY, WORCESTERSHIRE
DECEMBER, 1929

CONTENTS

ILLUSTRATIONS

I

WE ARE SET OUT

THREE MEN AND A STRANGE CRAFT

"PERILS OF THE TIBER"

A TEMPERAMENTAL RIVER

THE ALARM CLOCK

CHAPTER I

We Are Set Out

THREE men in a boat, not forgetting the sketch book. That, at least, is the romantic way of looking at it, for the boat consisted of a black rubber monster, inflated with much labour and with air; the passengers were our three selves, arrayed in a variety of colours, but on one principle in shorts and shirts; and the cargo comprised one sketch book, one pad, a number of pencils, four note books, three passports (to avoid arrest), three toothbrushes, one tube of toothpaste, a comb and brush, one cake of soap (at the time of writing it had not been settled whether we took soap or not), one pot of vaseline (to allay sunburn), a two-yard reel of adhesive plaster two inches wide (in case of punctures), a small roll of ordnance survey maps, and an alarm clock.

On the whole, we might well have supplied a sort of subsequent inspiration to Lewis Carroll to write "The Hunting of the Snark." You will see from the foregoing, for example, that even if we did have "forty band-boxes all carefully packed," "they were all left behind on the beach," though the fact that this book is now before your eyes goes to prove that in reality the Snark wasn't a Boojum after all.

To start at the beginning is always desirable in an early paragraph but, as a matter of fact, it is rather difficult in the present case, for it is almost impossible to realise that there ever was a beginning, unless it was in the distorted mind of the originator of the idea. But let us tell you a few of the things that happened to us before we actually reached the water—when, in fact, we were not quite certain that there would be any water, for Italian rivers have an uncomfortable habit of entirely drying up during the summer months —and then you will know just the sort of people we are.

Our vessel was known in Italy as a *canotto di gomma,* though why it should be known in Italy at all is a perfect mystery, for it was manufactured in America and purchased in a London store. Its external dimensions, when inflated, were seven feet in length by three feet in width; its internal measurements a little over five feet by about eighteen inches. When deflated, the whole outfit, including pump and paddles, was contained in a black bag that seemed to be about three feet both in length and diameter. The funereal aspect of the black rubber canoe and its black container was relieved by a white (originally) cord running round the gunwale, if one may employ so nautical a term for a craft that, we are convinced, became nautical only by necessity. Its main advantage was that altogether, including the divers accessories and the bag, it weighed only thirty-five pounds. The canoe defies further description; for a fuller appreciation of the frail craft, in which we faced the perils of the Tiber, you must rely upon our illustration. "Perils of the Tiber" we say advisedly, because sundry writers of travel books have an habit of describing the upper part of the river as invariably a raging torrent; this it is not by any means, at all times.

In Rome they will tell you the Tiber is not navigable above Orte. When one noble Roman matron heard that we proposed to start from San Sepolcro, twenty miles from the river's source, and traverse thence the hundred and ninety-five miles to Rome, she said, "Will you let me give you a little *conseil*? You take your canoe trip down the Tiber in your automobile." In England it was far worse. On all sides our friends predicted utter disaster and our sudden demise. They made us promise to send telegrams of our safe arrival at Rome, if we *did* arrive unscathed at the end of our mad adventure and, if we escaped with a mere puncture or two (hence the adhesive plaster), we were to consider ourselves jolly lucky. In short, it is more than certain that Lloyds would not have written our insurance.

At length we assembled in Florence preparatory to our departure for the upper waters of the Tiber. If you ask, "Why Florence?" we can only reply, "Why not? Florence is a very charming place." Arrived there, three things still remained to be done—to have a carpenter make a duck-board to put in the bottom of the canoe, to give it a name, and to launch it in the water.

If we could have read the carpenter's thoughts when he came to take measurements for the duck-board— that is, if the expression of the face is any indication of what goes on within—we are sure we should have had a name for our floating home. The carpenter made a very good job of the duck-board; the christening we decided to postpone till such time as a peasant should make some remark about our craft that tickled our fancy and suggested an appropriate name. In any case, we had decided that we dared not break a bottle of champagne over it, in the orthodox way, for fear of punctures.

As for the launching, we changed our plans on the very day before setting out. As we have said, we *had* intended to embark at San Sepolcro, but this was when we first planned the trip much earlier in the season. Two considerations now set us against this. One was that there seemed to be absolutely no direct means of communication between Florence and San Sepolcro by which we could transport our canoe; the second and really more important was that, even if we could easily have got there, it seemed certain that so late in the summer we should not find enough water in the river to float our craft. We therefore decided to take the water at Perugia, some forty miles farther down stream.

This change was somewhat of a disappointment, for Geoffrey and Frank knew nought of the Tiber valley above Perugia, and it is a rare bit of country far too fine to be missed without sincere regret. But we had the *canotto di gomma* on our hands and, under the circumstances, it had to be allowed to dominate the situation. Our original plan of beginning the cruise at San Sepolcro we could have carried out, under ordinary conditions, in April or May; had we attempted it in late August, we should have spent most of the time in carrying the canoe instead of it carrying us. And carrying a canoe for long distances over the boulders of a nearly dry river bed is no joke. As it was, we were by no means certain that late August would give us enough water for navigation even at Perugia. We were going there largely on faith and starting our journey with the spice of uncertainty. Indeed, some friends in Rome, who usually spend much of their time in summer on the river, had declared the undertaking impossible, even from Perugia. They looked upon our project as sheer madness.

Father Tiber is a very temperamental river and the constancy of his conduct is not to be depended upon—certainly not above Orte, at any rate, and not too much from Orte to the sea. One day he can be tame and harmless, pursuing his way in a perfectly hum-drum manner without the least sign of fuss or disturbance. The next, he can be a raging torrent, letting loose all the unbridled destructive violence of a giant on a rampage. He has never been a tractable agent, ready to be harnessed and lending himself kindly to the occasions of men. This is probably one reason why so little attempt has been made through all the centuries to turn his powers to account for the behoof of dwellers along his banks. He can be an agreeable enough companion, so long as you accept him as he is and fall in willingly with his changing moods; run counter to them ever so little and you bring down trouble on your head.

He is imperious, wayward and willful, and will brook no restraint. Those who judge him only by what they can see from the windows of the trains between Rome and Florence, know him not at all. The dull and slovenly appearance he presents to folk on the trains is only one of the aspects he assumes to shew his lordly indifference to human opinion. Gazing at him from the train, perhaps you think him sluggish; get on his waters and try to row or paddle against his current, and you will quickly discover the speed and force of his movements, likewise the baffling complexity of the cross-currents that beset you in every reach of his windings.

To know Father Tiber in his true character, you must follow his course from his rugged birthplace in the heart of the high Apennines, past Perugia and through the Umbrian plain, through Il Forello and the mountain fastnesses between that savage gorge and Orte, and accompany him thence till he has finished his meanderings in the Campagna, past Rome, and on to the end of his career at Ostia. Then, if you are a sympathetic student of river-psychology, perhaps you will understand something of his many-sided nature. If you have not yielded to the glamour of those mystic and little-known parts of Italy through which much of his seaward journey lies, and if you have not conceived a genuine affection for him, you will at least have learned to hold him in profound respect. *Father* Tiber you can fitly call him; you instinctively feel that he is far too august and reverend ever to be familiarly alluded to as "Old Man River."

When we say, then, that we decided to take the water at Perugia, considering the capricious and variable character of the upper river, you will understand that the unknown quantity in our calculations was holding us in suspense till we should see with our own eyes whether Father Tiber would graciously vouchsafe us the means of completing the expedition we had planned.

We are still in Florence. Before we start on the next stage of our faring, let us invite you to take one good look at our luggage. Most of it is self-explanatory. The reason for its scantiness is, of course, to be found in the dimensions of the canoe which, being like a modern house, barely allows room for three to squat in it. One article in particular, however, we must mention—the alarm clock.

Nobody knows why it went down the Tiber; in fact, nobody knows why it went at all. It was bought in London for 3/11, travelled out to Italy loose in the back of the car and then, one day, presented its luminous face to ours and, like most alarm clocks, demanded attention. In a flash we had seen it. We would leave our watches behind and take our alarm clock with us. Why we should want a clock, or any time-keeper at all, on so irresponsible a journey we were not quite certain, but we had decided. The clock would go along. We would fix it to the prow as a figure-head. It would, at least, be a means of readily distinguishing the prow from the stern, for in shape they were exactly similar.

II
DUCKS AND DUCK-BOARDS

AN UNRESPECTABLE CROWD

CHECKS AND CHECKING

CHAPTER II

Ducks and Duck-boards

EVERY musical comedy must comply with a recognised structural form—a first act, designed to put the audience in good humour by its originality; a second that ends on a note of seeming tragedy; and a short third act, in which everything turns out for the best.

The curtain rose on the first act when we descended from the hotel omnibus at the station at 6.20 on a hot, sunny morning typical of August in Italy. Harold was a gentleman down to the waist, and Heaven knows what below; Frank was really far too respectable to be included in the party at all, having shunned khaki shorts in favour of an elegant pair of white linen trousers that were made for him in Capri and never did fit, and a shirt that included all the colours ever used by Turner; and Geoffrey, who made no attempt to look anything at all, was distinguishable by his bare legs. He was one of those Englishmen who is always referred to as a "mad American."

Italians are always ready to be amused, and to shew their amusement, so that when we appeared,

Geoffrey dangling our mascot, the alarm clock, from one finger, the comedy began in good earnest. In fact, were the whole truth known, we should not be surprised if the "one night stand" we gave that morning at the Florence station were not in the end responsible for the fact that the Rome train started fifteen minutes late—a lucky thing for us, as you shall see.

Tickets were purchased amidst giggles and guffaws, and then we proceeded to the second act. This was to have opened with the checking of the duck-board, but many a good shew has had to be gagged on the first night. The Italians have unusual ideas on the subject of luggage. For example, they will allow you to take a large portmanteau into the compartment with you, but will be adamant in their opposition to a piece of three-ply wood, be it only four inches in width, because it is six inches longer than the portmanteau. So we had been fore-warned to check the duck-board and have it put in the luggage van.

This task was assigned to Harold, as he was the only one who could speak Italian, and the only one who didn't understand it until a sentence had been repeated to him twice or thrice, which was an admirable way of ensuring that one should do all the talking. In a few minutes he came back. It had been indicated to him that the duck-board could not be checked and put in the van. So we decided to try to steal through the barrier with the duck-board concealed as far as possible under the gentlemanly part of Harold's attire. Needless to say, it was discovered and we were stopped.

Harold returned to the baggage room, and Frank and Geoffrey settled down to await the result of his bargainings. There were twenty minutes remaining before the departure of the train. Ten minutes later, Frank went in search of Harold and came back to tell Geoffrey the news. The authorities considered the duck-board *freight*, which could not travel by a passenger train, but would have to go to Perugia by a goods train and would get there four days later. When the situation was explained to them, however, the geese turned into ducks and became most helpful and obliging. To take the duck-board along with us, nevertheless, would require special permission from the station-master and the filling out of sundry forms and documents. Frank and Geoffrey settled down to wait, leaving Harold to his negotiations. When the hand of the clock reached 6.55, the game seemed to be up. Frank and Geoffrey resigned themselves to the 9.37, and a tragic curtain fell on the second act.

When the hero, who has gone overseas to make his fortune, is stranded on a desert island, while the old home is being sold up for taxes, we feel the sheer hopelessness of the moment, but we are somehow sure that in the third act the impossible will happen and the hero will be landed once more on his native heath, just as the auctioneer's hammer is falling for the last time. Probably an air-ship has appeared out of the blue, or a submarine come up for air, and afforded a providential means of transport in the nick of time.

So, just as two of our number were considering the fate of the rejected, half of Harold—the top half—silhouetted against the duck-board, appeared through the barrier and shouted. We hastily collected our bits and pieces, dropped them, collected them again, and dashed for the train. We need not have dashed for, as we told you before, it started fifteen minutes late. And so on to Perugia, with a change at Terontola, where no untoward incident occurred.

III

THE UPPERMOST TIBER VALLEY

CASTLES AND FORTRESSES

AN UNSPOILED LAND

THE STORY OF ASSAI BRIDGE

THE LEAP OF THE BEAUTIFUL LADY

CHAPTER III

The Uppermost Tiber Valley

W E ACTUALLY launched our *canotto di gomma* at Perugia, it is true, and through sheer force of water conditions and the time of year our navigation began there. But it would not be treating Tiber with due respect casually to take all his previous course for granted and ignore the surroundings of his infant career. To complete the picture, then, we shall make a digression to the sources and take up the narrative of adventure again when, in natural order, we reach Ponte San Giovanni, the village lying at the foot of Perugia's hill, where the road crosses the river.

In doing this we are not indulging in needless description. It is safe to say that almost nobody ever penetrates into the uppermost part of the Tiber valley. It is a remote region, difficult of access, and quite out of the usual path of tourist pilgrimage. Even the Italians themselves, when they travel in their own land, seldom turn their journeyings thither. There is a little narrow-gauge line of railway across the mountains from Arezzo to San Sepolcro, a motor-bus connexion between Urbino and San Sepolcro, and a not very inspiring or satisfactory sort of branch-line railway, with semi-occasional trains, up the valley from Perugia. None of these modes of approach can be said to offer much inducement to explore, and most people who travel in Italy are very like sheep anyhow. They nearly all follow along the beaten lines they know to be frequented by other travellers. Though an increasing number travel by motor, and thus by road see vastly more of the country than they could ever possibly see travelling by rail, they still stick mainly to the well-known routes and rarely display enough initiative to strike off independently over little-used mountain routes to make discoveries for themselves. And thus it is that both the upper Tiber valley, and its sister valley, the Casentino, just across the mountain barrier to the west, have remained almost wholly unknown.

A distinguished French author has well said that few foreigners who pride themselves on their knowledge of Tuscany have more than the vaguest notion of the Casentino because they usually avoid the wild mountains and the forests that characterise this region; within a short distance of Florence, they miss much of the most glorious scenery imaginable, where Nature has showered gifts with lavish hand, to say nothing of the wealth of historical association bound up with the ancient castles and fortresses, or the treasures of art to be found in remote churches, treasures that have remained intact from the time when the monks were building their convents high in the mountain fastnesses while the valleys below resounded with the clash of arms.

What he has said of the Casentino, he might equally well have said of the valley of the upper Tiber, a mountain-girt land of wondrous beauty, forgotten by travellers and known to few. It is a land wholly unspoiled, and full of a peculiarly fresh and virile charm. You are away from the sophistication of museums; the enrichments of art are by no means lacking, but you will find them in village church and wayside shrine.

High up near the stern, bleak top of Monte Fumaiolo, twin springs gush from a bed of grey rocks and tawny sand. Thence their stream falls into a boulder-strewn grove of gnarled and ancient beeches. From just such a mystic spot can you not picture the river-god appearing and saying, as he rises,

. . . . . Ego sum . . .
Caeruleus Tibris, coelo gratissimus amnis?

Not far away a wind-swept pass over the ridge bears a road that descends into the Romagna and travels on to Rimini as its goal. All round are forests of oak and beech, or upland pastures regal with patches of purple heather or golden broom, where the mountain folk tend their herds and flocks. Two little villages, Le Balze and Falera, shelter in the lee of frowning cliffs. From one vantage-point near by you can see distant Camaldoli and the rock of La Verna, for you are in a lofty corner of the land of Saint Francis.

Amidst such unconfined and rugged beauty the infant Tiber begins his long descent to the sea, gathering strength as he goes from tributary rills that pour their offerings into his rocky bed. These same gentle rills become boiling, angry torrents when the snows are melting or after one of the sudden tempests that so often sweep the high Apennines, and their swollen streams account for the Tiber's temperamental bursts of flood and fury that are likely to break forth at almost any time.

Here and there bridges span the stream, and occasionally the youthful turbulence of the river is kept in harness long enough to drive a mill. To appreciate fully this region, you must get to know the people and their straightforward kindliness. You must learn the local legends and traditions associated with nearly every feature of the countryside and handed down from one generation to another.

The *Assai* Bridge, for instance, will remain more

vividly fixed in your memory when you know the
story of its building, which also throws light on the
fickle disposition of the river. Not far above Pieve San
Stefano, on a little hilltop, stands a ruined castle.
Just below the castle, five arches of heavy masonry
carry a narrow, steep-pitched camel-back stone bridge
of mediaeval aspect across the river-bed. Normally one
arch would suffice to span the water; the rest of the
bed is dry boulders. But when Tiber suddenly rises in
tempestuous violence after a mountain storm, the five
arches are none too many to cross his wrathful current.
This bridge perpetually recalls the memory of a drama
of love and sudden death enacted long ago.

Tradition has it that once upon a time there lived
in the castle on the hill a widowed countess with her
only son. Every night the lad came down the hill and
waded the river to go and pay court to the girl with
whom he was in love, who lived on the farther bank.
One dark night when there was no moon and the river
was swollen, the boy was swept away by the treach-
erous current and drowned. The poor mother shed
many a bitter tear and then, at the place where her
son had been drowned, she caused this bridge to be
built so that like misfortunes might not happen again.
When the bridge was finished, she looked at it and

said, "You have cost me Enough; you have cost me
the life of my only son." From that day the people
have called the bridge *Assai* (Enough). The peasants
will all tell you that on dark stormy nights, when there
is no moon and the wind goes wailing through the
forests, the waters of the Tiber run in demoniacal
eddies and you can hear under the arches of the bridge
the laments and long-drawn sighs of the bereaved
countess and her drowned son.

Not a few of the incidents of valley legend are of a
tragic character in keeping with the wild nature of the
scene where you almost expect to meet witches or
sibyls. In the neighbourhood of Valsavignone are the
Precipice of the Shepherdess and *Il Salto della bella
Donna,* both named for tragic episodes connected with
those grim, towering cliffs. The unhappy shepherdess
of the story was famous for her golden voice. From
dawn till dark she used to sing as she watched her
sheep and went spinning wool on her distaff. She was
as happy as the day was long. But her betrothed jilted
her to marry another. Thenceforth she became mel-
ancholy and sang no more. Leading out her sheep one
morning very early, she climbed to the top of a lofty
rock and putting her rosary around the neck of a
lamb, she cast herself off to her death. Abandoned by

its guardian, the lamb stayed on top of the rock, bleating. A mountaineer saw it and, going to investigate, found the lifeless body of the shepherdess at the foot of the crag.

The Leap of the Beautiful Lady, at no great distance from this place, is a sheer precipitous bluff overhanging the Tiber. The lady of the legend was so beautiful that few, it was said, could compare with her. In obedience to her parents' wishes, she had just been married to a young man of this neighbourhood and was accompanying him to her new home. Depressed at leaving the smiling plains where she had spent her girlhood, and overwhelmed at the thought of being condemned to live and pine within these awful solitudes, her reason completely failed her just as she came to one of the most terrifying declivities. Still wearing her bridal veil and garland, she spurred her horse to the edge and leapt into the abyss.

If the austere nature and solitude of this lofty valley have stimulated the tragic strain in the imagination of the mountaineers, it does not mean that they are morose or by any means lacking in joyous, wholehearted merriment. They are a cheerful as well as a kindly and simple people, and when they gather to celebrate a *festa*, no occasion could be marked by more genuine and spontaneous jollity. That the serious things of life have cut so deeply into their conscious-ness is merely the natural result of being closely hemmed in on all sides by awe-inspiring scenes and the sterner phases of the physical phenomena.

IV

PIEVE SAN STEFANO AND THE MOUNTAIN TOWNS

AN ANCIENT ROMAN SETTLEMENT

ITALIAN LIFE FROM A CAFÉ SEAT

MICHELANGELO AND ST. FRANCIS

A BACKLOG HINT

CHAPTER IV

Pieve San Stefano and the Mountain Towns

PIEVE SAN STEFANO is the first town of any size along the Tiber's course. Encircled by mountains as by an aureole, it lies in a green bason, its rich verdure, its flower-studded fields and the rapidly flowing river all combining to give it an engaging aspect of freshness and youth.

Yet, notwithstanding its general air of youthful vigour, Pieve San Stefano is a very old place. It is said to have been established as an ancient Roman settlement of woodcutters who felled trees on the nearby slopes and supplied building timber to Rome, binding the logs into rafts and floating them down the Tiber in the springtime when the river was in flood. We know that the Romans of the Republican era got a great part of the wood needed for their temples and houses from the immense forests that covered the Massa Trabaria, that high, steep country to the east of Pieve San Stefano.

Near Pieve, under some of the old bridges, can still be seen traces of enclosures or barriers which seem to have been made long ago to facilitate the timber transport down the waters of the Tiber on the spring freshets fed by the melting Apennine snows. Behind these enclosures the logs were lashed together into rafts and then, when the waters were at their full height, the rafts were pushed out into the stream and started on their way.

Pieve San Stefano in the dim past was called *Suppetia* or *Sulpitia*. Just when or why it got its present name is a matter of conjecture. One story has it that when the body of Saint Stephen was found under the ruins of a tomb at Cafarmagala, in the time of the Emperors Honorius and Tiberius the Younger, the people of Sulpitia, filled with religious zeal and enthusiasm, dropped the primitive name of their town and thenceforth called it in honour of the Proto-Martyr. According to another account, however, the name was bestowed on a different occasion; and thus it was. There was a certain rich man of the place, named Stefano, who had fallen into the Tiber and was being carried away by the swift current. Many citizens saw the mishap but, in spite of all their efforts to succour their fellow-townsman, they could not get to him. In his desperate need he called upon his namesake, Saint Stephen, to aid him. Thereupon he was miraculously dragged to the bank by an unseen hand and, as the Latin chronicle concludes, "evasit incolumis." In

Church of the Madonna dei Lumi
Pieve San Stefano

thanksgiving for this signal mercy, he turned his own house into a church to perpetuate the memory of this miracle. The people of the town, greatly moved by this timely intervention, put themselves under the protection and patronage of Saint Stephen, abandoned the name Sulpitia and adopted the new name, Pieve San Stefano.

Pieve San Stefano possesses no famous "sights." On the walls of the Palazzo del Comune and the Palazzo Pretorio are a number of medallions and armorial devices, both in carved stone and in polychrome maiolica, and there are sundry ancient terra-cottas and carvings in the various churches, but none of sufficient fame or importance to attract tourists. Perhaps, however, it might be a vastly good thing for their own sakes did more tourists now and then visit such places and take time to use their eyes and brains and to analyse the fundamental character and charm of Italian towns. Cut off from the hectic dissipation of "doing" museums, picture galleries and "sights" at top speed, they might possibly realise that every town has a subtle atmosphere of its own which it takes leisurely observation to appreciate.

And for just such leisurely observation of the little everyday incidents in the life of a town, the commonplaces in the occupation of the people, and the hundred and one small happenings that go to make up the corporate existence of the community, no point of vantage can be better than a seat outside a café in the corner of a *piazza* or market-place. There you can study to your heart's content the sundry local types and habits, the general quality of the architectural setting, and all the sequence of events and doings that enter into the local drama, so that you can get a true perspective if you possess at all a seeing eye and an enquiring mind. Quite apart from the individual personages who pass across the stage of the marketplace and play their parts, there will be such occasions as the weekly market with all its varied interest of colour and form, the divers wares exposed for sale, the motley throng it brings together, and the endless little by-plays of human nature it calls forth; perchance you will see a wedding procession pass or, it may be, a funeral cortège, each with its own characteristics of distinctly local observance; and, should you happen to be there at the right season, you might witness the procession on the feast of Corpus Domini when all the confraternities, habited in their traditional garb, march through the streets in due order with the clergy.

In such cities as Florence, for instance, far too many tourists are hustled from museum to museum and from gallery to gallery, and then whisked away again before they have had a chance to realise what manner of place they have been in. They have not been able to see the wood for the trees. Without in the least under-valuing either the interest or benefit to be derived from museums, galleries and "sights," we venture to submit that many tourists, who leave Florence with the inevitable impression that it is chiefly a sort of glorified shew-case, might gain a more reasonable and truthful conception of a very august city if they were occasionally allowed or took time, armed with a glass of *strega* and a plate of *biscotti*, to sit for a while in the Piazza del Duomo or the Piazza Signoria, and absorb the atmosphere, observing the everyday aspects of the place and people.

Pieve San Stefano, besides its regular weekly markets, has stated cattle markets or fairs when herds of the great long-horned white cattle, that play so important a rôle in Italian wayside scenery, are brought into the town to be sold or exchanged amongst the *contadini* of the surrounding region. The mountain country all round Pieve San Stefano is a conservative region where old manners and customs have remained unchanged. More than likely at one of these cattle markets you will see flocks of sheep, brought in from their pastures amid great groves of oaks, in the care of robust peasant women still wearing the old-fashioned

shaggy broad-brimmed hats and scarlet cloaks characteristic of their calling hereabouts.

Besides seeing traditional modes of dress, you will
probably discover that many curious customs are still
preserved among the hill people. For instance, it is
still their habit to carry a new-born infant to church for
baptism covered with a red cloth or robe, if it is a
boy; with a white cloth, if it is a girl. The parents of
the woman in child-bed visit her, bringing a present
of hens and eggs. Weddings are celebrated with salvos
of shots as a salute of joy, and with fireworks or bon-
fires, while as a symbol and happy augury of con-
jugal fidelity for the newly-wedded couple, the
friends and wedding guests prepare what are called
serragli. These are long streamers or ribbons of silk
which they wind round and round the bride and
groom before the marriage-party enters the parents'
house on the return from the church.

In the long winter evenings, the young men of the
countryside often gather at parties at the houses of the
more well-to-do farmers; to indicate that the party has
lasted long enough and that it is now time for the
swains to go home, the mistress of the house moves the
backlog of the fire and pushes it from its position on
the hearth.

In this same mountain region, in the months be-

tween May and November, on moonlight nights you
can often hear the melody of lusty voices floating down
the valleys. They are the serenades of the young blades
who are singing rounds and catches under the windows of their sweethearts—old rounds and catches,
full of sylvan vigour and freshness, which their fathers
and grandfathers sang before them, and which they
now sing with the same ardour.

Not far away from Pieve San Stefano is the little
town of Caprese. It is not directly on the Tiber but beside the Tifi, which pours into the Tiber its trickling
rill or its torrent, according to the time of the year or
the state of the weather. At Caprese are the ruins of an
ancient stronghold, and the battle at which Totila
was defeated is believed to have been fought in the
immediate neighbourhood. Be that as it may, authentic
documents of Caprese's history go back to 1082. What
is of interest to most persons, however, is the fact that
it was the birthplace of Michelangelo. His father,
Ludovico di Lionardo Buonarrotti Simoni, was *podestà*
of the two castellated villages of Caprese and Chiusi
for the Commune of Florence. Here, under the walls
of the old castle, Francesca di Miniato del Sere bore to
her husband, the said Ludovico di Lionardo, the son
Michelangelo whose name was to become famous

throughout Christendom. This was on the 6th of March, 1475.

The little house of the *podestà* in which Michelangelo first saw the light of day is still standing; so also is the tiny church of San Giovanni whither they carried him for baptism. To the wall of the house is now affixed a marble tablet with this inscription:

QUI

IL VI MARZO DEL MCCCCLXXV

A

LODOVICO BUONARROTTI-SIMONI

PODESTÀ DI CHIUSI E DI CAPRESE

PER IL COMUNE DI FIRENZE

NACQUE DA MADONNA FRANCESCA DEL SERE

UN FIGLIO CHE FU

MICHELANGELO

E L'ANNO MDCCCLXXV

IL COMITATO FIORENTINO

NELLA ESULTANZA DEI POPOLI

CHE ABITANO

FRA LE FONTI DELL'ARNO E DEL TEVERE

QUESTA MEMORIA

A INAUGURARE LA CELEBRITÀ CENTENARIA

IN NOME D' ITALIA

PONEVA

There can be little doubt that the wild, haunting beauty of this rugged corner of Tuscany must have impressed itself indelibly on Michelangelo's consciousness amongst the vivid memories of childhood. There can be little doubt, too, that the rugged vigour of his character owed something to the natural qualities of the land of his nativity. Had he been born in the plains of Lombardy or in the arid flats of Campania, it would be hard to imagine him shying a paint brush at the Pope's head when the pontiff looked into the Sistine Chapel to see how the decoration was coming on—and that without respect to any hereditary bias in his temperament.

Caprese has, too, its treasured memories of Saint Francis. Thrice, they say, he passed near by and paused on his way to or from La Verna: once in 1214, when the demons beat him with rods while he was praying in a mountain chapel during a furious tempest; once in 1218, when he stopped to rest in the church of Zenzano; and the last time in September, 1224, when he was leaving La Verna for the last time on his way to Porziuncola to die. Then it was that he stopped on top of Montarcoppio hill, near Caprese, whence he could look back at La Verna and said: "Farewell, mountain of God, holy mountain, mountain of sacred bonds, mountain of peace, mountain in which it hath

well pleased God to dwell. Farewell, Mount Alverna;
God the Father, God the Son, and God the Holy
Ghost bless thee; rest thou in peace, no more shall
we see each other."

On this hill the people of Caprese built a chapel
whither pilgrims still go in throngs, despite the steep
and difficult ascent. Of all the saints in the calendar,
there is none for whom the people of all this country
cherish a more genuine and beautiful affection and
feeling of friendship than for that far-seeing humanist
and truly gentle man, the blessed Francis of Assisi.

About twelve miles southward of Caprese stands
Anghiari on its hill above the Sovara, one of the
Tiber's many tributaries from the enclosing mountain
slopes. Anghiari is really a dual town; there is the old
or upper town within the ancient fortress walls, and
there is the lower town of more recent building. The
latter is unalluring with its decorous uniformity of
houses and its decorous and dull monument to Garibaldi, one of the first of that numerous crop of marble
monstrosities to be set up in Italy after the Risorgi-
mento. Garibaldi may have been a very admirable and
gallant patriot; his bronze and marble effigies are
abominable nightmares. The only attraction the lower
town of Anghiari can boast is its view over the broad-
ening out of the Tiber valley.

Quartiere dei Lanzi
Montauto

It is altogether different with the old or upper town. There the streets amazingly steep, crooked and narrow; the tall houses, piled up one against another at various angles and appearing anxious to huddle close together for protection in a time of peril; the old doorways, the lower windows with great iron grilles, the steep steps; the stone carvings, the beautiful remnants of wrought ironwork, and the venerable towers at the gates all combine to form an unspoiled and complete setting of typical town life in the Middle Ages.

Besides the interest attaching to the upper town as a dramatic and highly picturesque *ensemble*, there are many excellent specimens of architecture and not a few good paintings, terra-cottas and sculptures to be found here and there in the places they were originally intended to fill. Anghiari is not a place of concentrated art pellets, otherwise known as museums, which the speedy tourist doing Italy on schedule time can gulp down in so many minutes and then be off again. It is a place that reveals its charms only by degrees, and even then only to the traveller who is willing to walk about and use his eyes. Not the least reward that Anghiari has to offer to anyone making a circuit of the walls is the marvellous view thence, commanding the vast barrier of the central Apennines in the distance with Monte Fumaiolo and the Alps of the Moon, while below is spread out the Tiber valley from Città di Castello to Borgo San Sepolcro with its *campanili* and towers, the stream, now past the impetuous descent from its lofty source, winding placidly through the green plain between rows of tall poplars.

It was beneath the walls of Anghiari, on the 29th of June, 1440, that the allied armies of Florence and of Pope Eugenius IV put to rout the army of Filippo Maria Visconti, Duke of Milan, led by his *condottiero* Niccolò Piccinino. To commemorate this notable victory of the Florentine and Papal forces over the Milanese, Leonardo da Vinci was commissioned to paint the Battle of Anghiari on the walls of the Sala del Consiglio in the Palazzo Vecchio.

Not many miles to the west of Anghiari are the ruins of the Castle of Montauto, a place whose associations leave an indelible mark on the history of the upper Tiber valley. This mountain fortress was built of old and occupied by the Counts Barbolani of Montauto until it was dismantled in 1503 by the Signoria of Florence. Since then it has fallen into utter ruin, save a few remnants preserved on account of their association with Saint Francis.

Saint Francis came to Montauto in September, 1224, when he had left La Verna for the last time. He was weary and ill. Count Alberto di Ranieri Barbolani re-

Cloister in the Convent of the
Cappuccini, Montauto

ceived him and offered him food and shelter. Then, when he learned that the saint had been warned by God to prepare himself for death, and that he was then on his way to Santa Maria degli Angeli where he expected soon to end his days, the count begged of the blessed Francis that he would leave some memorial of his visit before he went away. Grateful for the hospitality, and having nothing else to give, Saint Francis left his habit, the same he had worn when he received the *stigmata*. Until the castle was dismantled nearly three centuries later, this habit, wrapped in a covering of silk and gold, was an object of veneration in the chapel of Montauto.

When the Florentines "slighted" the castle, they took this relic of Saint Francis to Florence where it is still treasured in the church of Ognissanti. The memory of Saint Francis, however, has always remained green on the hill of Montauto and the poor mountaineers deeply cherish his association with the spot. The *quartiere dei Lanzi* or Guard Room of the castle is preserved and kept in repair because it is the tradition that Saint Francis lodged in it.

V

BORGO SAN SEPOLCRO AND THE TOWNS OF THE VALLEY

A PEAR-SHAPED VALLEY

ITALIAN ENGINEERS

THE BELLS

PIERO DELLA FRANCESCA

PLINY'S ESTATE

CHAPTER V

Borgo San Sepolcro and the Towns of the Valley

THE plain of the upper Tiber valley is shaped like a wedge or—better still—like a pear, with the large end to the north. Beyond that, the course of the river is narrowly hemmed in by steep mountain slopes, coming ever closer and closer together, until you reach the source high up on Monte Fumaiolo.

At the upper or northern end of this valley plain, where it is about five miles wide between the feet of the towering Apennine spurs that completely surround it, lies Borgo San Sepolcro just underneath the eastern mountain range beyond which are the Marches and the Adriatic coast.

San Sepolcro's rail and motor-bus connexion with the outside world we have already mentioned. Aldous Huxley calls the rail line across the mountains from Arezzo a "low-comedy railway." As none of us has ever entered the Valle Tiberina by that means, we cannot testify to its shortcomings from personal experience. Having encountered comparable transportation futilities elsewhere, however, we can quite credit any amusing aspect of equipment and operation that he or

61

other travellers may have discovered; but for the
engineering of this, or of any other Italian railway, we
can feel only the profoundest respect. Difficulties seem
merely to stimulate the Italian engineers' ingenuity;
they never block the fulfillment of any scheme. To
balance any comic quality or any discomfort that may
attend this rail transit from Arezzo to San Sepolcro,
there is more than ample compensation in being able
to feast all the way on that "clear beauty of the Tuscan
hills, that have something not Tuscan about them."
The opalescence and soft glamour hanging over the
heights that shut in the upper Tiber valley are more
than the figments of mere imagination.

The motor-bus route from Urbino to San Sepolcro
does some amazing climbs and descents and brings
you into the little city at the foot of Monte Maggiore
through one of the most beautiful of the lateral valleys.
As for the railway line between Perugia and San
Sepolcro, it has no such physical difficulties to sur-
mount as the line from Arezzo, but nevertheless it
seems to arrogate to itself the privilege of consuming
as much time for a given distance over a comparatively
level course as the Arezzo line does for traversing for-
midable grades.

Take it all in all, when you consider the nature of
the public facilities for access to San Sepolcro—beyond

which none of them extend—it is not hard to understand why this somnolent old valley town and the region round about it are so little disturbed by the general run of travellers.

The upper Tiber valley can scarcely be called sparsely inhabited. The many little hillside hamlets and the ruins of mediaeval castles perched on crags within sight of San Sepolcro would dispose of any such impression, even were the farmsteads and villages dotted about the flat lands of the valley left out of account because they are less readily visible. Indeed, there are few parts of Italy not well-peopled, despite occasional appearances to the contrary. That explains why it is so easy for a crowd to collect quickly, springing up seemingly out of the ground, even in remote places. Of such a non-obtrusive population San Sepolcro has long been the centre and, though small and sleepy, the city has all the presence and self-assurance of ancient establishment.

Encircled by its battlemented brick walls and now useless moat, this little, drowsy metropolis composedly overlooks the fat cornfields and vineyards of the plain, while olive orchards clothe the lower slopes of its mountain background. Silent and respectably dingy Renaissance *palazzi* and houses line the streets. Here and there graceful wrought-iron balconies, or other

items of decorative amenity, arrest the admiring gaze.
The dominant feature of the *piazza* in the centre of
the town is the *campanile*. This tower, along with the
neighbouring palaces and churches, could doubtless
tell many a beguiling tale of the days when Borgo San
Sepolcro was a self-contained and independent little
republic, with its own nobility, its own usages, and
its own political aspirations.

The *campanile* is an isolated structure and is quite
independent of any church or other building. Fashioned of cut stone, it was built by the people many
centuries ago at the height of their civic pride, both as
bell-tower and an ornament to the city, and from
dawn till dark the bells still ring merrily forth on
every possible occasion. When you come to think of it,
it is really astounding how much individuality there is
in bells and bell-ringing throughout Italy. Used as we
are to the peals and the well-ordered traditions of bell-
ringing in England, perhaps we are apt at first to be a
little contemptuous of what seems to be the harum-
scarum jangling of bells in Italian towns. But hearken
patiently and eventually you will find something like
order emerging out of chaos and, before you know it,
you will find yourself becoming fond of what you first
regarded as nothing but a cacophonous din.

The bells are unmistakably different in tone from

English bells. They are not so mellow and, as a matter
of fact, some of them are positively harsh and raucous.
Not a few of them are cracked and hoarse, and sound
as though they were just about to lose their voices
from old age. But, in some subtle way, they fit into the
picture as nothing else could and you would miss them
terribly were they silenced. The method of ringing—
or, perhaps, you prefer to call it the *lack* of method—
differs in every city and town. Venetian bell-ringing
is not to be confounded with Florentine bell-ringing,
any more than the note of the Marangona could be
mistaken for the voice of the major bell of the Duomo
in Florence. Roman bells, again, are every bit as individual in tone, and the manner in which they are
rung, as are the bells of either Florence or Venice.
Whether it be the Marangona's deep-throated crash
that sends Saint Mark's pigeons circling upward from
the Piazza, or whether it be the snarling roar of the
great bell in Giotto's tower, with all the lesser bells of
Florence following in chorus, Italian bell-music adds
much to the complex charm of the land. At San Sepolcro the *campanile* and bells make a very characteristic
feature of the town, and one is glad to hear the metallic clangour as many times a day as it pleases the
ringers to pull the ropes.

Borgo San Sepolcro is not heavily starred in the

guide-books. Baedeker disposes of the whole situation with the summary assurance that "hurried travellers may see the points of interest in about two hours." We willingly concede Baron Baedeker's reliability in the matter of maps and the bald statement of facts; we submit, at the same time, that his judgement isn't worth a straw on the score of aesthetic values. Let the omniscient Baron and his "hurried travellers" scamper through San Sepolcro just as fast as ever they like; for our own part, we are convinced that anybody "doing" the place on a time limit, with a list of "sights" to be ticked off in transit, will be disappointed and had better not go there at all. On the other hand, if they are willing to browse about, they will find not a few diverting things to repay them besides sundry compensating incidents of architecture and picturesque odds and ends, in addition to the Romanesque bas-relief frieze of mounted knights, beasts, dragons and birds on an ancient façade, which is the only fragment that seems to have impressed the callous imagination of guide-book compilers.

In the eyes of the art-loving world, of course, San Sepolcro's chief claim to fame is that Piero della Francesca was born there, in 1406, and that three of his most notable paintings, including the Resurrection, are still preserved there. Piero seems to have been in some measure an exception to the rule that a prophet is not without honour save in his own country. The San Sepolcro Brotherhood of the Misericordia in 1445 commissioned him to paint an altar-piece for their chapel; this was the *Madonna della Misericordia*. This altar-piece and the *Resurrection* are both of them now carefully treasured in the Palazzo dei Conservatori. The *Infant Hercules* is in the Palazzo Collachioni. Besides these paintings by Piero della Francesca, the town possesses divers other gems of painting and terracotta, but the gloriously triumphant *Resurrection* alone is well worth making a long pilgrimage to see, although Baron Baedeker gives it only one star when it ought to have three.

From San Sepolcro the Tiber meanders peacefully through its narrowing valley to Città di Castello at the southern apex of the wedge, augmented by several mountain tributaries as it goes. Its sinuous course is marked by poplars, oaks and a continuous growth of water willows; here and there are long reaches of smooth water between the boulder-strewn shallows which become boiling rapids when the stream swells into its frequently recurring floods. Between the well-tilled fields, on both sides of the river, the vines are often festooned from tree to tree in a manner to suggest very vividly that the swags and drops of Classic

decoration were first inspired by this ancient practice
of the peasant farmers.

Città di Castello was the old Roman municipium of
Tifernum Tiberinum where Pliny the Younger had
an estate which he mentions in his *Letters*. On one
occasion he writes: "Hail has ruined the crop in my
farm at Tifernum Tiberinum. From my tenants at
Como I hear of better prospects, but of low market
prices. My Laurentinum alone seems to be right, but
what do I own there? A cottage and a garden surrounded by sands!" Pliny's villa at Laurentum, of
which he speaks so modestly as the least of his three
estates, has been described by archæologists as really
an establishment of considerable importance. We may
imagine, therefore, that the place at Tifernum Tiberinum, about which he takes no such deprecatory tone,
was an estate of a size and value befitting one of the
conspicuous public characters of Imperial Rome under
Trajan.

Tifernum Tiberinum, we know, was both proud
and wealthy and commanded all the commerce of the
rich and fruitful valley of the upper Tiber. Its population in Imperial times was far larger than now, and
it was a place of so much account that the Goth Totila
deemed it worth while to turn out of his way to sack

and destroy it. Città di Castello as we see it to-day is
a walled town of the Renaissance. Its massive brick
battlements rising abruptly from the flat surrounding
plain were built in 1518; most of the moat that once
encircled them has been filled up.

During the Renaissance the Vitelli family were the
lords and masters of Città di Castello and they still
own not a little of the land in the neighbourhood.
Fortunately for the townspeople, the Vitelli "tyrants,"
as it is the fashion to style the absolutist leaders of the
period, were enlightened and beneficent princes, generous patrons of the arts and as keenly possessed of the
building mania as any of their contemporaries. Indeed, the town we now know is mainly the result of
their constructive ambitions. The different Vitelli
palaces are amongst the most notable buildings the
visitor will find, but the many charms they disclose
will not occupy him to the exclusion of the Duomo,
the Palazzo Comunale and a number of the parish
churches, all of which deserve attention either for their
architectural and picturesque merit or for the art treasures they hold. Then, too, there are endless incidents
that beguile the eye, too unimportant in themselves to
be enumerated as "sights," but none the less contribut-
ing substantially to the town's pleasant character. And,

as an unfailing source of interest, there are always the
people and all the small happenings of everyday life
in the streets and *piazze*. Città di Castello is a most
agreeable place to browse about in, making discoveries
for yourself, and being thoroughly irresponsible in the
disposal of your time.

From Città di Castello southward to Umbertide—a
distance of about fifteen miles—the Tiber valley is
much narrower, and though there is still a tract of
level plain highly cultivated, through which the river
winds beneath its rows of oaks and willows, the opposite lines of mountains now stand almost toe to toe, so
that this stretch of the valley is like the neck of a
bottle. Umbertide, though actually a very old town, is
rather modern and commercial in appearance, and
apart from its famous old castle, guarding the valley
from an eminence, and a few buildings dating from
the Renaissance there is comparatively little to induce
the traveller to tarry.

All through this narrow neck of the valley from
Città di Castello to Umbertide you become more fully
aware of its well-peopled state from ancient times. On
every hand are farmsteads on the slopes, fortified hillside townlets clustering round their churches, monas-
teries or pilgrimage shrines, or the ruins of mediaeval

castles perched on the more commanding sites. For
an artist in quest of dramatic and compelling studies,
or for an holiday a-foot, it would be hard to imagine
more captivating country.

From Umbertide the next eighteen miles of the
Tiber's course lies through what at times is little more
than a gorge, so closely do the mountains and hills
hem it in. You are conscious of a profound change
and you realise that you are leaving this pleasant "land
apart" with its memories of Saint Francis and Michelangelo, of Piero della Francesca and that amiable
"Conservator of the Tiber," Pliny the Younger, to say
nothing of the mediaeval lords of the land who fought
and loved and built brave castles and wove their
strands into the complex web of history and romance.
The road and the narrow-gauge railway accompany
the river through this long gateway. The river hastens
on, now through still-flowing reaches, now over stony
shoals and rapids. There is the same dusty old highway over which Roman legions and mediaeval *con-
dottieri* have marched, along which merchants and
princes, sinners and saints have travelled, the same
dusty old highway that bore the river company for
untold centuries before the railway thrust itself in as
a partner in the traffic. Thronging memories of the

long drama of the past come unbidden as you make
your way through this ancient thoroughfare, but above
them all you are keenly aware that you have left behind you a definitely distinct phase of the Tiber's life
and that before you lies something wholly different.

VI

PERUGIA AND ETRUSCAN REMAINS

APPAREL ETIQUETTE

AN ITALIAN VISTA

THE CULTURE OF THE ETRUSCANS

CHAPTER VI

Perugia and Etruscan Remains

FROM the narrow, eighteen-mile gateway that guards its upper valley, the Tiber comes out into the plain of Umbria beside the foot of Perugia's hill. Perugia is so well known and has been described so many times that we have no mind to enter here into a further rehearsal of its glories. Besides, on this particular expedition, we had our own very good reasons for avoiding Perugia, much as we love the Umbrian capital and much as we delight to be there whenever circumstances permit.

To begin with, our habiliments were scarcely of the sort to make us feel at ease in walking through Perugia's streets. Italians very properly resent the easy and "superior" nonchalance with which certain *forestieri* parade the thoroughfares of their ancient and dignified cities, arrayed in the most unconventional and nondescript attire as though they were off on a camping trip in the wilds, and their behaviour sometimes quite in keeping with their garb. These same persons would not dream of walking the streets of London, New York or Paris coatless and hatless, and

wearing plus fours or shorts. Italy may be a trifle
warmer in summer than the cities just named, and
they may be off for an holiday and feeling relaxed,
but these considerations do not at all excuse their appearing in the streets of Rome or Florence, Venice,
Bologna or Perugia in a sort of hooligan *négligé* they
would not tolerate for a moment in their own homes.
As we thoroughly agree with the Italians on this point
of apparel etiquette, we preferred to avoid Perugia.

In the second place, Perugia is on a lofty hill while
the Tiber, quite naturally, is in the valley below.
When we were headed for the Tiber and, moreover,
particularly anxious to see whether there was going to
be enough water for our enterprise, a diversion into
Perugia just then would have been about as pointless
as the famous expedition of the French king with
forty thousand men, "who marched them up an hill,
and then marched back again."

So bent were we on reaching the river, settling our
fears about sufficiency of water, and putting our prob-
lematical India rubber craft to the proof that we not
only stayed in the train past Perugia and right on to
the station at Ponte San Giovanni, but we also sternly
repressed our archaeological hankerings and left the
nearby Etruscan tombs unvisited.

And all this resolution we exhibited even though, at

that time, Geoffrey had never been in Perugia and Frank had never seen the Etruscan tombs. To let anyone pass Perugia or the Etruscan tombs seems little short of criminal. Under ordinary circumstances such conduct would have been absolutely indefensible, and if we had admitted it we should also have hung our heads in shame and accepted the revilings of our friends without a murmur. But an India rubber canoe, as yet untried; a river waiting to try it on; the momentous question still to be settled whether we could all three get into it after we had blown it up and launched it; and the itching expectation of all manner of strange adventures ahead—these were extenuating considerations sufficient, we trust, to excuse our avoidance of Perugia, even had we had suitable raiment to go there —which we hadn't.

As a matter of fact, it is just about as bad to "do" a place like Perugia in a scurry of indecent haste as it is not to go there at all. There is little choice in the degree of iniquity attaching to either course of conduct. Sometimes, indeed, it seems as though the traveller who deliberately passes by is less to be blamed and less to be pitied than one who hastily dashes in and hastily dashes out, and goes away with a blurred notion that the town is a collection of art exhibits in a rather extensive museum. In any event, the traveller who goes by escapes a false impression, and he has the compensation of a pleasure to look forward to at some future time.

Anyone who knows and loves Italy cannot help being filled with mingled resentment and pity that so many visitors apparently regard Italian cities and towns as well-staged museum exhibits instead of as living organisms full of vitality and replete with every phase of human interest. All the past glories of art and architecture are inseparably bound up with the corporate life of the people, and any conception of Perugia, or of any other city or town in Italy, that merely takes account of the gems of architecture, craftsmanship, painting or sculpture as isolated incidents, without including the complete setting and the many-sided aspects of the local life of to-day, is bound to be dead, miserably poor and misleading.

It is all very well to lavish admiration upon the many glorious paintings and frescoes enshrined in the various buildings; the Palazzo Pubblico, that masterpiece of secular Italian Gothic tinged with the approaching mode of the Renaissance; the fountain in the stately Piazza between the Palazzo Pubblico and the Duomo, a marvellous creation designed by Bevignate and sculptured by Niccolò and Giovanni Pisano before the end of the thirteenth century; the Collegio del Cambio with its frescoes by Perugino and its amazing craftsmanship in carving and intarsia; the exquisite polychrome façade of the little church of San Bernardino of Siena, or innumerable other individual features of wondrous beauty. But if you fail to co-ordinate these single works in the whole setting, of which they are inseparable parts, or to envision them in their relation to both the past and the present full-flowing life of the city they adorn; if you fail to see in the Corso Vanucci anything more than an avenue leading to duly listed "sights" to be seen; if you fail to grasp the manner of life the people live; if you fail to explore some of the steep side streets dropping mysteriously downhill beneath ancient archways, and winding between the beetling fronts of mediaeval palaces; if, finally, you fail to linger again and again on the parapets of the city walls and let the magnificent views of the Apennines, and over the Umbrian plain at your feet, sink so deep into your consciousness that you can never forget them, your memory of Perugia will be as dead as a dodo and mean little more than the confused recollection of a dream.

If you cannot explore Umbria to the full limit of your wishes, you cannot do better than survey it from the vantage point of Perugia's walls. The panorama there unfolded before your eyes will give you at least

some measure of the mystic glory that enfolds the
land. To the north and east the Apennines pile up, tier
above tier, clothed in gradations of colour so subtle
that no words can do them justice; westward lies
Lake Trasimenus, its lofty background of hazy blue
mountains beyond; to the southeast Assisi glistens on
the lower slopes of Monte Subasio, a vision so tenderly
lovely in the rays of the westering sun that it almost
hurts to behold it; southward the Tiber winds through
the western arm of the Umbrian plain to distant Todi
proudly seated on its hill. Towards every point of the
compass, it will more than repay you to take the outlook in the varied and ever-changing lights of morning and late afternoon. Don't be satisfied with a view
at only one time of day; endless variations are at your
command.

For such a proper taste of Perugia as we have just
outlined, there was no time. With our arduous programme ahead of us, and our lack of suitable clothing,
you can understand why we were obliged to sacrifice
Geoffrey's education for the nonce and list Perugia for
his later efforts. To forego this pleasure Geoffrey was
the more ready as he professes not to like sight-seeing.
In actual fact, he enjoys and appreciates sights and
scenery just as much as most people do, only it is fatal

to suggest that he does or to make any allusion to the subject.

You may not be an antiquarian—you probably are not—and you may be devoid of any pronounced archaeological hankerings but, all the same, if you are at Perugia you ought not to miss going to see the Tomb of the Volumnii which is only a short distance from Ponte San Giovanni. That expedition Frank also, as well as Geoffery, had to miss, so exigent was our anxiety to get on the river or *in* the river—it really mattered very little whether *in* or *on*, as you will soon learn.

Besides the Tomb of the Volumnii, there are various other important Etruscan remains in the neighbourhood, but the burial place of this Etruscan family who lived at Perugia some twenty-five centuries ago is readily accessible and is probably the one that will most vividly impress the average person who is not a professed archaeologist. It is hollowed out of the living rock and is a complete specimen of the corridor tomb in its most perfect development.

After gaining entrance by descending a flight of steps, there is a central hall or corridor from which open out nine chambers. The roof is carved to simulate a wooden construction of beams and rafters. Two of the nine chambers contain burial urns; the rest are empty. All of them, however, are adorned with sculptures and mural reliefs. To come down from the dazzling sunlight and enter this dim chamber of sepulture, where you see the effigies of men and women whose features proclaim their connexion with the generations living in the same place to-day, makes an indelible impression on your memory and forcibly convinces you of the abiding unity of Italian history and civilisation, notwithstanding all the ephemeral turmoils, conquests and confusions that have filled so large a space in the chronicle of events. When you dip a little into the story of the Etruscans and their brilliant culture, and remember that many of the hill towns to-day are exactly the same in shape and size as when the Etruscans first surrounded them with walls; that not a few of these walls, indeed, incorporate the remains or, at least, the foundations of Etruscan walls; and that no end of Christian churches stand on the foundations of Etruscan temples, you begin to realise what a potent factor in Roman civilisation were these pre-Roman teachers of Rome in the arts of peace.

It is not only round about Perugia that we find abundant traces of Etruscan culture and occupation. There is scarcely a place along the whole course of the Tiber where you may not pick up at any moment some stray bit of Etruscan bronze or terra-cotta. The

Roman matron who counselled Harold to "take the canoe trip in an automobile" once gave him a beautiful little Etruscan terra-cotta lamp that had just been dug up on one of her estates near Città di Castello and dutifully sent to her by the *fattore*. Again, another friend who had been shooting in the river valley, once grasped a tussock of grass to help pull himself up a bank and felt something metallic in his hand. It turned out to be an exquisite Etruscan bronze statuette —probably washed out of the soil by a downpour of rain and caught by the tussock.

And so it goes. You never know when you may chance upon a treasure of this sort in the most unexpected place. The Etruscan guardian spirits, or our patron saints, as the case may be, did not favour us with any such mementoes in kind of our expedition— our patron saints probably thought they had quite enough of a job to look after our madcap selves—but we were constantly reminded, in one way or another, of the long-departed Tuscan and Umbrian masters of this fair land.

VII

THE FIRST PLUNGE

PONTE SAN GIOVANNI

FITTING INTO THE CANOE

MUD AND WATER: ROCKS AND RAPIDS

CHAPTER VII

The First Plunge

ARRIVED at Ponte San Giovanni, though it was only eleven o'clock, we sought luncheon at the station restaurant. This was no case "where every prospect pleases." In fact, the restaurant looked more like a third-rate wine-shop than a place where meals could be supplied. However, at the magic word *mangiare* all was changed. A clean tablecloth and snow-white napkins appeared, and we had quickly before us the inevitable but satisfying *pasta al sugo*, peaches and a bottle of red, or as the *padrona* preferred to call it *black*, wine of the countryside.

Our equipment, which we had left outside, was already occasioning much interest, and when we were ready to move off a small crowd had collected. News travels in Italy with more than electric rapidity. The "mad Americans" were coming as veritably as the Campbells—and from that moment forward we had our admiring audience, always of small children, but often of adults as well, ever ready one and all to be of any assistance they could. It made you feel that you ought to scatter *largesse* in the grand manner.

The village of Ponte San Giovanni offered us nothing very startling to inspect and we made off at once in the direction in which the Tiber lay. Besides, we were anxious to discover if there was to be any water.

We could not have discovered a more delightful place from which to embark. There *was* water! And on our left lay an old mill, its walls shining in the sun and reflecting those cool colours that only old age can produce on stone and stuccoed walls. Just below us, spanning the stream was the *ponte vecchio*, an old stone bridge, shaped like the hump of a camel, with six unequal arches and rising to an height of about forty feet in the middle.

While Geoffrey and Harold were blowing up the canoe and preparing it for its launching, Frank sate down to sketch, and as we called backward and forward to each other, we were excitedly informed by the small members of our audience that three of their number also bore the name of Francesco, which was quite to be expected in this land of Saint Francis.

At last all was ready, and we carefully packed our various paraphernalia in such parts of the canoe as were most likely to be safe from water, an hopeless attempt as we were soon to learn. Twelve-thirty saw us afloat and, in some miraculous manner, all three of us fitted into the canoe—we employ this term for lack of another name, for our craft resembled a canoe about as much as it did an Atlantic liner. It looked far more like the Graf Zeppelin almost entirely submerged. We were quickly to learn that she was never intended for three.

We started with no great stir, beyond chatterings on the part of the crowd who now began to move off downstream to await our advent. Wait they certainly had to. We paddled out hopefully into the stream, and passed under the bridge. Then we pulled in to the farther bank. We had come to our first weir.

We paused now to consider the lesson of the first hundred yards. In order to embark, we had found it necessary to stand in the water; to disembark we were forced to step into the mud. Obviously, the first necessity was to remove our shoes and stockings as they brought more mud and water into the canoe than we thought desirable. In fact, we removed them quicker than we had intended, for Geoffrey slid on his face as we carried the canoe across the slippery breast of the weir on which it was quite impossible to stand up with shoes on, rubber-soled or otherwise. This caused a slight delay as Harold, having removed his stockings, felt he must apply more vaseline to his calves. Fortunately, our audience was still with us and they assisted us with the canoe to a point where it seemed convenient to re-embark.

But not for long did we remain comfortably seated. Ahead of us lay the new bridge of Ponte San Giovanni and, just before it, we were to have our first experience of Tiber rocks and rapids. The rocks were arranged in an inconvenient manner in parallel bands running diagonally across the stream, so that there was no one clear channel. It was necessary, therefore, to lift the canoe from one channel to another. In these channels were rapids caused by boulders of various sizes lying just below the surface. The last of the channels ran at about the speed of a mill-race and with equal force. The only thing to be done was to let the canoe go down alone; the submerged boulders were too numerous and too near the surface to let the canoe get by with any weight in it at all. It was accordingly shoved off on its own. Geoffrey had gone on ahead to catch it as it passed under the bridge and hold it till Frank could get far enough down stream to catch it again. Just as it reached the bridge, it swerved sharply to one side. Geoffrey made an effort and caught it, but he reckoned without the depth and strength of the stream. There was a splash, and the next thing the others saw was a face grinning above the waters. The first plunge had been taken.

VIII

WE LEARN TO WALK

CHAPTER VIII

We Learn to Walk

GEOFFREY said that he would not have minded the immersion at all if only the canoe had not bumped him so hard on the rocks. In fact, the water was very pleasant and from that time onwards Frank and Geoffrey were always in and out of the water, and the difference rapidly disappeared between Frank's presentability and Geoffrey's lack thereof.

Harold was far more staid and refused to enter the water, at any rate above the knees. His excuse, a flimsy one, was that there were two things he must keep dry —the capital of the party, and an Italian Government permit which allowed him, to use his own expression, to stand on his head within or without any building in Italy. This he rated much higher than our passports, which he was carrying also and was willing to submerge in the waters of the Tiber at any moment.

Started again, the next two miles of our journey were an almost unbroken succession of rapids, and we were heartily glad we had not attempted the descent from San Sepolcro. After these two miles, the river widened a little and there were quite good and navi-

93

gable stretches between the rapids. Frank and Geoffrey soon found that walking on the stones—under water or out of water—without shoes was even worse than bringing a lot of water and mud into the canoe, so to shoes they returned.

It was immediately necessary to devise some satisfactory means of propelling the canoe. We had started with the two paddlers in the bow and stern respectively, and the observer in the middle. This did not prove an altogether successful method, as the boat shewed a marked tendency to go round in circles. A *canotto di gomma*, as we soon discovered, cannot be paddled with the same ease as an ordinary canoe because of the fact that the gunwale measures about a foot in width, it is rounded at both ends, and there is not the least vestige of anything resembling a keel. A further difficulty was that Harold had theories, the chief of these being that whatever happened the paddlers should keep stroke and paddle at a regular rate. This regular rate he proceeded to stick to, regardless of the eccentricities of his companion in paddles, and regardless of the eccentricities of the craft.

At most rapids it was necessary for one, if not two, of us to get out, while the remaining one or two attempted to guide the canoe. Occasionally we would shoot a rapid with all three aboard, and great would

be our delight thereat. For most of the two miles of
rapids Frank and Geoffrey were in and out of the
water, leaving Harold hopelessly at the helm because
of his seeming aversion to getting wet.

At last we had passed the worst of the rapids and
reached the smoother waters. We still had not entirely
lost our audience, though the personnel had changed.
It was as though word of our coming had gone before
us, for every little while we would find fresh faces
peering at us in astonishment from behind the trees
or from between the bushes that lined the river on
both banks. We know now exactly what must have
been the sensations of Hudson and other explorers as
they voyaged along unknown rivers closely watched
by the curious natives. On their side, the Italian peasants were probably quite as much amazed at our India
rubber craft as ever were the American Red Indians by
Hudson's sails. At twenty minutes past two a tragedy
occurred. Our mascot, which had by then imbibed a
little too freely the waters of the Tiber, ticked its last.

Even in the smooth water our progress was not fast,
and Geoffrey had a new idea. The water was fairly
deep and he would swim behind the canoe. This, he
opined, would enable the others to paddle the vessel at
a faster rate when it had been lightened by an hundred
and seventy pounds. To accomplish this, he somewhat

foolishly abandoned his shoes. All went well until the water became too shallow for swimming, and his progress was slow and painful over the stony bottom of the river. To catch up with the fast-retreating canoe, he went ashore and climbed the bank, finding at the top a cart track along which he could run.

When he caught up the canoe he found that Frank and Harold were dissatisfied with their present method of propulsion. Apparently the front seat sagged too much to make paddling comfortable—the seats, it should be mentioned, were strips of rubber stretched level with the top of the canoe. The canoe was, strangely enough, fitted with row-locks. We had, at first, mistaken them for handles to pick it up and carry it by, but when we discovered that they were not placed at the point of balance, their true nature lay revealed. We decided, therefore, that Harold should row the boat while the other two walked (or ran, as speed demanded) along the bank. This process the runners did not at all enjoy, for their legs were scratched by brambles and they had no diversion ex- cept the sight of a woman husking Indian corn. To watch Harold, however, was a circus in itself. He rowed quite unaffected by the behaviour of the canoe. If she was stern foremost, he rowed forward; if she

preferred to go bow foremost, he rowed backward.
Nevertheless, he got there.

Ever since leaving Ponte San Giovanni the banks on
both sides of the river had been almost without exception fairly high. And both shores were well grown
with poplars and acacias, with occasional groves of
sycamore or oak between the river and the fields or
vineyards beyond, while a dense shrubbery of water
willows overhung the stream and dipped their
branches in the water. Under the circumstances, from
our low position we could see little or nothing of the
country through which we were passing as we worried
along, rowing, paddling or pushing by fits and starts.
The only glimpse of visible habitation along this reach
of the river was the village of Montebello, perched on
a low hill about a mile and an half to the right. This
Geoffrey caught sight of during one of his pedestrian
diversions along the bank. It looked a typical hill village with no especially outstanding features.

Throughout its entire course, there are very few
towns directly on the Tiber. The river runs through
Pieve San Stefano; it runs past the foot of the hill on
whose top Perugia sits aloft; it runs past Ponte San
Giovanni whose houses come down to the water's
edge; it flows through Rome, and it flows through
Ostia where was its ancient mouth. Otherwise the

Tiber towns are nearly all more or less remote from the stream and generally perched high on their dominating hilltops. Their builders placed them thus in troublous ages for purposes of defence. It is often said, too, by way of explaining this customary exalted site, that people believed the river level unhealthy. It is much more likely, however, that the notion of defence was uppermost in their minds and that therein is to be found the true explanation.

Ultimately, when Frank and Geoffrey got back into the canoe after their sundry perambulations on the bank, a new method of procedure was adopted. Harold and Frank sate in, or rather *on*, the stern and Geoffrey rowed. This was not very satisfactory because paddles are not oars, so a new and final scheme was then devised. It was really so obvious that we were surprised we had not thought of it before—the two sitting at the stern should paddle. This last arrangement worked wonderfully well until we ran amongst some snags. Harold and Frank shouted, Geoffrey leant over the front and tried to fend them off, but his effort was too late.

There was a bump, a pop, and then the sound of escaping air. Harold and Frank pulled for the shore. Fortunately there was a rock-covered sand-bank near by. To get the front of the canoe out of the water as soon as possible and keep the forward air chamber from being flooded, Geoffrey jumped into the water himself, but he did it too rapidly and Frank thereupon was tumbled neatly out of the back. Harold, as dry as ever, brought the sinking craft to land.

It requires a great man to be able to laugh at himself and, perhaps, we may be forgiven if at the moment we considered the matter serious. In retrospect it was, of course, extremely funny. If you can, imagine a tyre floating on water and becoming deflated, but only at one end, and three people sitting in it. The one jumps out, and a second falls out, (not an unfunny sight in itself), and the third goes serenely on until his command has reached port, like a captain sinking with his ship—it *is* funny.

Once ashore, we examined the damage. It was not so bad as it might have been. There was a slit in the front end about an inch long. We got out the adhesive tape that we had thoughtfully carried for just such emergencies. Like all things that had been in the pockets of either Frank or Geoffrey, it was quite sodden. We were therefore mistrustful of its water-proofing qualities. We put on three thicknesses over the puncture and blew up the canoe. It shewed an unmistakable tendency to leak. We decided, accordingly, to make for the nearest village and have it mended. By this time the sun was near setting, so we could have it done overnight.

On enquiry from some peasants staking down hemp to rot in the river, we discovered, as we had imagined, that we were about two miles from Torgiano on the left bank of the stream. We had come ashore for repairs on the right. Geoffrey went across to reconnoitre; Frank brought the boat carefully down stream; and Harold, risking all, walked across the river. He wet the bottoms of his shorts!

In one of his peregrinatory essays, Aldous Huxley says "it is practically impossible to travel without being sometimes bored" because part of the traveller's time is empty and unavoidably spent "in merely getting from place to place." While it is often undeniably true that the "merely getting from place to place" is boresome, in our passage from Ponte San Giovanni to Torgiano we could certainly not complain of being bored for a moment, even though the riverside trees and herbage prevented us from seeing anything of the land immediately on either side of us. Between the manifold vagaries of the temperamental Tiber and the vagaries of the craft in which we had elected to travel, we were too much and too diversely occupied to be bored. There wasn't time to be bored. There wasn't time even to think about being bored. As a sure pre-

ventive of *ennui* we can heartily commend a Tiber
journey in a collapsible India rubber craft such as ours,
the only kind of craft, in fact, in which more or less
continuous navigation of the upper river is possible.

Torgiano, in the manner of most towns and villages
along the course of the Tiber, as we have just pointed
out, crowns an hill, and so we had to climb, carrying
the canoe with us. Geoffrey estimated the distance as
half a mile from the river, but half an hour later he
admitted his errour. As we trudged along a lane bor-
dered by mulberry trees, there were little groups of
women and children in the fields on either side; the
children were playing and the women were just fin-
ishing their work for the day. In one group there
were two Umbrian Madonnas eating watermelon and
very deftly managing to do some needlework at the
same time. Just afterwards, the cart track we were following led us through a typical Umbrian farmyard.
It was a rough square, partly paved with stone flags
on which lay great piles of Indian corn that had just
been hulled; farmhouse, hay-ricks and barns formed
the boundaries of the enclosure. Wherever you go in
Umbria, in late summer or early autumn, you will
see golden bunches of Indian corn on the cob tied to
farmhouse walls or to every branch and twig of trees
nearby, hardening and becoming more golden in the

air and sunshine until it is ready to be hulled. In some of the fields, where early autumn ploughing was in progress, the wooden ploughs of ancient pattern were often drawn by as many as three yoke of great white oxen. In the hedges the ripening haws were turning a deep crimson and the romantically-named bittersweet was taking on the full glory of its mature colour. Behind us the sunset was crystal-clear, pale blue and yellow, and green and rose, in all the exquisitely tender hues we see in the primitive Umbrian paintings.

IX
TORGIANO

THE BLACKSMITH MENDS THE CANOE

THE FASCIST BARBER

CLEANLINESS IN ITALY

TORGIANO'S MARKET-FAIR

DERUTA AND ITS MAIOLICA

CHAPTER IX

Torgiano

AFTER a last sharp ascent, at the entrance of the town the usual admiring throng met us and, when we let it be known that we had a puncture to be repaired, they led us forthwith to the blacksmith. If you have been in remote and little-visited parts of Italy, being taken to the blacksmith for a puncture repair will not surprise you. The blacksmith is usually the handy-man of every village and a person of diversified accomplishments. He is the mechanic, the electrician, sometimes the carpenter and, of course, the blacksmith. We were not sure that a functionary of such universal prowess would wish to bother with so trifling a thing as a puncture, but mend our puncture he did, both cheerfully and well. He even offered to put our too-bibulous alarm clock to rights and make it go again, but we decided to make him a present of the alarm clock.

Having commended the *canotto di gomma* to the care and protection of the blacksmith for the night, our next thoughts were very naturally directed towards food and accommodation. There was, of course, no inn and in so tiny a town where tourists of any sort were absolutely unknown, accommodation of any sort seemed unlikely. However, one small boy volunteered to find us food and lodging and marched us off to the other end of the town, with a following crowd of his playmates, all deeply interested in our appearance and our doings.

Having interviewed one old woman, who was unable to give us shelter, we came at last to a sort of general provision store and *trattoria*. The *padrona* said she could give us rooms and she thought she could feed us, but on the latter subject she would have to consult her husband when he came home. So we sate ourselves down and consumed a bottle of wine while waiting. When the husband appeared, he decided we could not be fed as he had not what he considered the necessary wherewithal to get us up a proper meal.

Under an increased convoy, which must have numbered all the children and some of the grown-ups of the place as well, back we started to the opposite end of the town again in quest of food, having settled only one half of our problem. Again we were unsuccessful and still another small urchin bobbed up with a fresh suggestion that he thought he could find someone to feed us in almost exactly the same place we had just come from. Just as we were beginning to picture ourselves spending the night going round in endless circles in search of dinner, an angel appeared in the guise of the local Fascist representative.

Many kind things and many hard things have been said for and against the Fascist movement but, be that as it may, we invariably found the Fascist representatives in the small villages extremely helpful, and not only *willing* to be helpful but actually on the lookout to be so. Everywhere you go in Italy it has always been our experience that the people, high and low, rich and poor, have been kindly, courteous and hospitable, especially to *forestieri*. Their thoughtfulness and their desire to be helpful are evidenced in a thousand different ways; their good offices are perfectly spontaneous. But the local Fascist representatives in each place add to this natural and unorganised good will a sort of organised responsibility and watchfulness for the reputation of their several towns and villages.

Our particular young Fascist in Torgiano was a barber in ordinary life. Immediately grasping the situation, he came up and offered us his assistance and then bade us wait for a moment, while he disappeared into a neighbouring private house. We had not long to wait, for which we were not sorry as we were getting very hungry indeed and every minute of uncertainty only sharpened our appetites. When he

reappeared it was to tell us the welcome news that a
meal was already in course of preparation. We then
invited him to join us in a glass of Marsala at our
lodgings over the way while our dinner was a-cooking.

This gave us a chance to ask him questions about
Torgiano. It was a town of between seven and eight
hundred souls, we learned, and was the market-town
for a considerable surrounding district. This we could
have a chance to see for ourselves as the next day was
market-day and all the booths would be put up in the
streets early in the morning.

As we had our Marsala in the room back of the
shop part of the *osteria*, we were, of course, causing
the usual excitement and attracting a throng of possible customers—a thing for which the landlord ought
to have been grateful to us, we thought, instead of
going into a funk at the idea of getting us up a dinner.
However, few strangers and no foreign travellers ever
go to Torgiano and this humble little *osteria*—the
nearest approach to anything at all resembling an inn
—probably had not the necessary equipment nor the
requisite victuals for doing what the *padrone* judged
a dinner suitable to the occasion, and there was no way
of finding them at such short notice.

Our interested followers were all anxious to talk to
us and to shew us their sundry treasured possessions,

just like so many good-natured children. One curious
thing they exhibited was a very dirty and ancient pack
of cards. The suits were swords, staves (or clubs),
pennies and cups, and the cards were numbered from
one to seven; then came knaves, queens and kings.
Every now and again in Italy you come across these
strange old packs of cards, quite different from the
modern sort, that have survived from the use of the
Middle Ages or the Renaissance and are still being
made.

After dallying and chatting a while over the
Marsala, and watching a game played with the archaic
cards, our Fascist friend led us across the street to our
dinner. An excellent repast it was, and mightily welcome, too, even though it consisted chiefly of the inevitable *pasta al sugo* and beefsteak done almost to a
cinder over the fire. The peaches were as hard as
bullets, but then bullet-like peaches and pears are the
most esteemed in Italy; if they were mellow and ripe
they would be regarded as quite *infra dig* and not at
all in proper condition to appear on the table.

Dinner over—and how much more comfortable and
happy we now felt!—we found our Fascist guardian
angel waiting below in the street for us, so we sate
down beside the potted bamboos outside the *osteria*
and treated him to a Marsala nightcap. This act of

courtesy and thanksgiving discharged, we were glad enough to betake ourselves to bed at the end of a very grilling day. When we had toiled up the steep hill into Torgiano we had been too tired and hungry to think much about what the place looked like, and now, when we had at last been fed, it was too dark to see very much, so we postponed our inspection till morning. Our rooms and beds were immaculately clean, a state of affairs, by the way, that you will almost invariably find wherever you go in Italy, no matter how humble the quarters, nor how unprepossessing they may look from the outside.

Bright and early next morning—almost before it was fully light, in fact—there were sounds of preparation from the booths that were already being set up in the street through the whole length of the town and in the little park beyond. The park was nothing but a dusty square area with low parapets and a few trees at the sides. Early morning noises in Italy are very obvious and always indicate exactly what is going on. They are likewise numerous and varied.

Torgiano possesses two streets that come together at both ends. One of them is comparatively straight and is probably called, if it is ever or anywhere named at all, either the Corso Vittorio Emanuele or else the Via Garibaldi, as these seem to be the favourite names in

Street Scene
in Torgiano

such cases. The other street, which is more or less of a secondary consideration in the scheme and has neither name nor any suggestion of the grand manner, branches off from the main artery at one end of the town, pursues its humble, curving way, and then swerves back at the other end of the town to rejoin the parent road again. Thus the street plan of the place is shaped very much like a drawn bow.

The bowed back street, without any pretence at grandeur, is nevertheless an attractive spot to loiter in if you are prone to sketching or if you enjoy watching human nature in homely, everyday aspects. For the artist's sketch book, there are inviting subjects without number in the shabbily picturesque houses whose outside stairways seem to have been contrived expressly as posts of vantage for pots of gaily blooming plants, small children and meditative goats.

Here and there fig trees or blossoming oleanders peep over the tops of old garden walls, while through the gateways you catch seductive glimpses of the orderly disorder of shrubs, trees and flowers that only long-neglected gardens can assume. Perhaps against a background of sun-flecked house-front you see a buxom, barefoot peasant lass, her locks restrained by a crimson bandana, striding past with the fine, free swinging gait of the woman accustomed to working in the fields and poising on her head one of the great copper Umbrian water pots or a wicker basket full of fruit, vegetables or even live chickens.

The skill some of these *contadine* shew in perfectly balancing loads both bulky and weighty on their heads is astonishing; they will go stepping along at a brisk pace, up hill or down hill, knitting a stocking or plaiting straw as they walk, never lifting a hand to steady the burden aloft—apparently, indeed, never even giving it a thought—and, of course, busily talking the while.

Like as not, another back-street life study you will find diverting will be some of the women sitting at the doors of their houses, their feet on the doorstep, their chairs tilted back in the roadway—there is no pavement—hard at work over their tambours doing the traditional Umbrian linen embroidery or making a piece of the famous Umbrian lace. Beautiful designs rapidly take shape under their deft fingers, and almost never will you see them looking at a pattern or anything to guide them. Their instinctive feeling and their familiarity with popular tradition are enough. Other local characters of all sorts, too, you will see passing by from time to time, each possessing some distinct interest.

One side of the street that is not continuously built

up, from the several intervals between the houses, affords long views over the valley below and across the
plain to the surrounding mountains, conical hills with
their villages atop standing out here and there in the
distance. Back-street rambling is generally an entertaining pastime and, taken altogether, the back-street
of Torgiano offers a variety of rewards quite equal to
those yielded by most places of the sort.

On this particular morning, however, our first interest was breakfast and, after that, a survey of the
town under the enlivening stimulus of market-day.
To get our breakfast we had to go foraging again,
very much as we had been obliged to do for our dinner
the night before, but as an Italian breakfast is rather
a trivial matter the job of discovery was not serious.
In a tiny, irregular piazza back of the church we
found a place that was part café, part general-supply
and draper's shop. Seated at a spindly and wobbly
iron table outside the door, we had a breakfast to be
remembered only for its badness and the melodra-
matic accompaniment going on inside—inside the
establishment, not inside our anatomies. We had very
nasty, lukewarm black coffee, and venerably ancient
biscotti of sickly sweetish flavour. Geoffrey said the
coffee tasted like spoiled absinthe. He ought to know
because he likes absinthe; Harold and Frank detest it.

As for the biscuits, they had "lain a long age," if not in "the deep-delved earth," certainly out of their tin. This repast we ate to the screeching accompaniment of a tearful quarrel between a young wife and her apparently uninterested and unresponsive spouse. In fact, the demonstration was all on one side and was staged behind the drapery counter indoors where the highly perturbed woman gesticulated and gave vent to her feelings with vocal volume and intensity worthy of a prima-donna. We thought it a pity that anyone gifted with such superlative lung-power could not have been trained to sing in *Die Walküre*. As one of the Valkyr maidens, she would have made the welkin ring without the least effort.

Along the Corso Vittorio Emanuele or the Via Garibaldi, or whatever the chief thoroughfare of Torgiano is named, there are several large houses that evidently once belonged to persons of quality and importance. One of them is a quite delightful Renaissance *palazzo* with a number of interesting details. Across the street from its main doorway, and obviously belonging to it, is an imposing brick exedra in the Baroque manner. The back of the seat is continued upward and forms a wall with a fantastically shaped top displaying scrolls and finial decorations; at the middle of the curve is an impressive gateway that admits to the private garden beyond. Architecturally Torgiano is otherwise devoid of any noteworthy features. The church and its bell tower are pleasantly picturesque but of no outstanding merit to attract attention.

On the morning of our departure the shady side of the town's main street was lined from end to end with booths containing everything imaginable from shoes, clothing, gay-coloured bandanas and dress-goods to garden-produce, mouse-traps, poultry and crockery. A rummage-sale would have paled into insignificance beside the diversity of wares this Torgiano market-fair put on display. There were, of course, oxen, sheep, pigs and goats for sale or barter, as well. The crockery was spread out at random on stands and on the ground, and some of the pieces coming from name-less and unfamed country potteries, and priced at only a few *centesimi*, were admirable enough in shape, colour and decoration to make us wish we could carry a little of this humble but distinctive ware along with us. The vivid consciousness of our cramped quarters in the *canotto di gomma*, however, effectually silenced any acquisitive longings.

The goods of the coppersmith were not less alluring than those of the potter. There were all sorts of im-plements and utensils from pots and pans, and the deep, slender contrivances they use for beating up *zabaione* in, to the big, swelling pots or jars for carrying drinking water from the springs and public fountains. These copper water pots, by the way, have strongly individual shapes, each one of them characteristic of some particular part of Italy. One shape is typical of Tuscany, another of Umbria, another of Lazio, and so on, and there is no possibility of mistaking one for another.

The people in the market were no less interesting than the wares displayed for sale. We saw one woman marching along with a basket on her head in which were two live geese, waving their necks about in time to the vibrations of her footfalls. Another woman looked like a walking poultry yard; she could scarcely be seen for the chickens she was carrying, not only in the large tray-like basket on her head, but suspended in a diversity of ways that no one but an Italian peasant could think of devising. Then there were watermelon vendors with their luscious fruit on little stands, temptingly cut into slices of just the right size and shape for picking up and eating on the spot. In the dusty park just beyond the end of the street, where most of the cattle selling and buying went on, one booth sheltered a barbecued pig, still on the spit on which it had been roasted whole, and now it was being sold slice by slice. And very toothsome it looked, too. Of course, there were the usual sweetmeats and pastries in abundance, at different stands, and the sweetmeat and pastry purveyors seemed to be doing a thriving trade.

The Italians may eat a nominally very small and, indeed, negligible breakfast, but we have often noticed that most of them are quite ready to begin nibbling various and sundry *bonnes bouches* quite early in the forenoon, so that, by the time the luncheon hour arrives they have not infrequently had the equivalent in quantity of a fairly substantial breakfast.

When we had finished exploring to our hearts' content we visited the obliging blacksmith, got the canoe which he had patched substantially, and started once more Tiberwards. We had decided to embark on a tributary of the Tiber, called the Chiascio, as it lay considerably nearer the town than the river and there was only a short walk down hill to reach it. Thither we were accompanied by about fifty of the villagers, most of them men and boys, with a trail of children tagging along. On our descent to the stream we were relieved of all the burden of carrying the canoe. Every one of our interested band of followers was anxious to get a chance merely to *touch* our strange craft; to be allowed to *carry* it they esteemed a signal privilege.

While we were making ready to start we were entertained by the sight of some of the small boys catch-
ing fish with their bare hands in the shallows. What
kind of fish they were we do not know, but they
seemed singularly stupid and inert to allow themselves
to be taken thus without effort. All along the upper
river we noticed frequent contrivances of small stakes
and brushwood—pounds or enclosures—which evidently had something to do with fishing, but exactly
what was the method of making the catch we never
discovered. These rude enclosures were often con-
structed near or actually in the boulder-strewn
stretches of rapids so that it was sometimes difficult to
avoid them when negotiating these obstacles to our
course. However, they added to the excitement of the
journey. These fishing pounds or traps and an occasional clumsy ferry boat, worked by an overhead chain
or cable, were almost the only evidences that the
dwellers along the banks had anything to do with
the river. All the other marks of man's intervention in
its affairs consisted of lengths of heavy wire netting,
filled with boulders and saplings, fastened by stakes
along the banks at different points where there was
danger of the cross currents and eddies causing serious
erosion when the stream was in flood and violent in
its course. Sometimes these protecting barriers of stone-

filled wire netting were replaced by walls of well-built stone masonry.

Across the Chiascio at the foot of Torgiano's hill is a picturesque old stone mill borne up by arches under which the stream flows with a full head of water. These ancient mills of the Tiber valley present varied aspects, all of them inviting you to linger and investigate. Frank wanted to sketch the mill at Torgiano, but we had spent so much time poking about the town itself that we felt obliged to put off for Deruta without further delay. As we paddled away, Geoffrey raised his hand to wave "Good-bye." Immediately from the bank fifty hands went up in the Fascist salute. The small boys followed us for a while along the shore, but fell off one by one before we reached the junction of the Chiascio with the Tiber.

The journey from Torgiano to Deruta was not marked by any undue excitements or untoward incidents. Nobody fell overboard and we had no punctures. This part of the river was unusually free of rapids and shallows and, for most of the distance, we had a smoothly-flowing stream with deep water to paddle on. It was mainly a case of plugging ahead steadily and getting over the miles. Incidentally, we got thoroughly well cooked, for the day was extremely

hot and still and the fierce reflection from the water
was like the breath of a furnace.

About two miles below Torgiano we passed under
the Ponte Nuovo which carries the road from Perugia
to Deruta and Todi. Like so many of the Tiber
bridges, it is a graceful structure and spans the river
at a great height. Of the six arches, the two central
ones are of stone and the two at each side of these are
of brick. The effect is agreeable. To enhance the interest of the composition, just by the end of the bridge
on the left-hand bank is another ancient mill, built
of mixed brick and stone used apparently at random,
set amidst a grove of tall, spiky poplars.

For most of the distance the banks were heavily
grown with water willows, while behind them were
often rows of oaks, sycamores and, occasionally,
clumps of dark cypress to punctuate the scene with
their sombre colour and incisive contour. Now and
again there were plantations of pine or rows of sentinel
poplars. Beyond, on both sides, the country stretched
away in well-tilled corn-land and vineyard, the vines
festooned from tree to tree along the boundaries between the fields. In the distance, at the edges of the
valley, the rounded lower hills were either crowned
with walled towns and villages, towers and old ruined
castles accenting their silhouettes, or else terraced with

that peculiarly characteristic precision that distinguishes Umbrian hillsides and gives them the appearance of being sharply combed.

All the way along, the river follows a meandering course and often makes great ox-bows so that the distant view of the hills and mountains is constantly changing at every rood of the journey. One moment straight ahead of you rises some mediaeval fortified town on its conical eminence, the mountain background swelling behind it in a farther-removed plane of the picture; the next, as the river sweeps round a curve, you behold a chequered vista of cornfields and olive orchards spread out on slopes so steep that you wonder how the *contadini* ever manage to do their ploughing. And all the landscape is wrapped in the veil of that tender, dreamy summer haze that is dreamier and hazier in Umbria than anywhere else. Time and again, at either side of the stream, stone-faced embankments and heavy stone jetties testify to the menacing force of the Tiber when the spring floods come rushing down the valley or when the river suddenly rises in boisterous wrath after a great summer storm in the mountains.

The sight of Deruta from afar, as you come down the river, makes one of those idyllic pictures that etch themselves indelibly on the memory and can never afterwards be dimmed. Set on its hilltop, the irregular line of its walls, its towers and its piled-up roofs is cut by the sharp accents of tall cypresses which seem to have an uncanny faculty of always rooting themselves just where they will add the fullest dramatic force to the composition. Up the ascent climb steep, toilsome roads that disappear from view within the shadow of high-arched gateways. All around are fields and vineyards and olive orchards that make a chequered setting of grey-green, golden yellow and brown, the intense brown of Umbria's soil in the pitiless blaze of high noon.

If you are at all a connoisseur in ceramics, or if you are a collector of pottery, the name of Deruta will send a thrill through your being. Deruta was one of the foremost Renaissance centres of maiolica-making and some of the choicest sixteenth century maiolica masterpieces were decorated there and fired in its kilns. From the sixteenth century to the eighteenth the wares of Deruta deservedly enjoyed high repute. Then, in the nineteenth century, the well of inspiration seemed to run dry. Within the past few years, however, the industry has taken on a new lease of life, and creative instinct and good taste alike have experienced a marked revival. To-day there are flourishing maiolica factories and the town seems to be in a fair

Deruta
from the River

FRANK A. WROUS.

DERUTA

way of winning back its old laurels. Many of the old models have been either copied or successfully adapted, and the old methods, that produced such wonderful results, are once more faithfully followed. Deruta pursues its beautiful industry untroubled by the outside world, for this ancient hill town is in a remote part of Umbria and access is difficult as there is no line of railway anywhere near. Consequently, it is not visited by tourists, especially as it has no notable "sights" to attract them.

As a rule, the only outsiders who go there are those who in some way or other are particularly interested in the design or manufacture of maiolica. Nevertheless, despite the fact that travellers know it not and rarely or never go there, Deruta is one of those many homely, pleasant, unpretentious places full of a peculiar kind of charm. Its attraction, apart from its highly picturesque quality, is the charm of those quiet, unassuming places whose people go composedly on, century after century, doing their duty "in that state of life unto which it hath pleased God to call them," and enjoying the beauties and the good things of their surroundings without sensational excitement. Deruta is a typical Umbrian small hill town, and without knowing such you cannot really know Umbria or Italy. It is just the sort of place that those of us

who know and love Italy best always delight in going
to and lingering in.

When we were come as near to Deruta as the river
will bring you, we lifted our boat out of the water and
left it in the shade of a great mulberry tree that grew
at one corner of a nearby farmyard, while we climbed
the hill into the town to get our luncheon. The little
farmyard was paved with big stone flags; at one side
was the farmer's house; on another was the barn; on
the third were the hayricks and stacks of straw; and
the fourth side was open to the road with only a low
hedge between. In other words, it was a typical small
farmstead and the farmer was a typical kindly Umbrian peasant who was quite ready to shelter our be-
longings for as long as we chose to leave them there.
Putting the canoe in the shade was a rather necessary
precaution for the sun was so hot that the cement of
the seams had begun to melt and we were afraid that
we should spring embarrassing leaks before the end
of our day's journey.

One of the roads up to the town ascends at a cruel
gradient and is entirely paved, or rather strewn, with
maiolica potsherds. It was not comfortable to walk
on, especially in thin rubber-soled tennis shoes, and,
what with the broiling mid-day heat, the rigour of the
grade and the sharp fragments underfoot, the only

thing we could think of all the way up was the line of
the hymn "they climbed the steep ascent to Heaven,
through peril, toil and pain." The only peril, of course,
was the possibility of our being reduced to nothing
but mere grease spots before we reached the top; the
toil and pain were there realistically in full abundance.

When you get within the walls there is seemingly
not one foot of level ground till you reach the piazza
at the very top. Not a few of the streets are nothing
but flights of steps, and these stepped streets go zig-
zagging about in the most mystifying manner. One
minute you are looking up at some particular house,
the next you are looking down on its roof. Here and
there, at intervals between the houses, these stairway-
streets have low parapets at the sides over which you
can look directly into gardens and orchards hanging
on to the steep slope of the hill or beyond to the river
and plain far below you and the mountains closing
in the horizon. With such views to be had for the
looking, it is not hard to understand how it is that
many Umbrians can be perfectly happy to lean their
elbows on their window-sills and just do nothing but
gaze over their glorious country for hours at a time.

Deruta is a cheerful place, and one of the things
that makes it of a glad and "cheerful countenance" is
the almost universal habit of putting out pots of

blooming plants from the windows, supported in little
iron rings bracketed out from the house walls. Besides
the cheeriness of the blooms themselves, the pots containing them exhibit an endless diversity of the most
graceful and fascinating shapes. Another factor that
makes for the cheerfulness of Deruta is the variety of
distant vistas you get at every turn, both from the
parapets and angles of the stepped streets and through
the arched gateways. There is no point of vantage
from which you can better survey the character of the
valley of the Tiber or better appreciate its beauty.

At the end of the piazza at the top of the town there
is a good Renaissance fountain whither come the
women and children to fill their copper water pots for
the home drinking and cooking supply. The thirteenth century church of San Francesco, farther along
the piazza is rather dilapidated on the outside but
within it is well kept and there are some interesting
remains of early wall paintings. The most noted is a
painting of God, the Father, surrounded by saints, by
Fiorenzo di Lorenzo, dating from 1475. In the Town
Hall are some other paintings and likewise a small but
rather fine collection of maiolica. These are about all
the listed "sights," but the chief charm of Deruta is in
the characteristics not noted in guide-books, the kind

of characteristics to be discerned only by actual contact with the place. And all of these are pleasing.

In Deruta lace-making and embroidery go on in the streets with as much activity as in Torgiano. The women sit at the doors of their houses with tambours they can hold in their hands, or with large frames that have to be supported on two chairs, and work away with a will, chatting with their next-door neighbours, who are doing the same kind of needlework, or with their friends who stop for a word of gossip.

As we had left the *canotto di gomma* in the farmyard by the river side, we had nothing but our clothes to recommend us to special attention in Deruta and, consequently, we were not accompanied by such curious throngs as our craft always seemed to collect. The only time we blocked traffic was when Frank sate down near the gate to make a sketch. This quite demoralised the lace-makers, the carters and any chance passers-by. They were all interested and appreciative and wished not only to have a look but also to stay and see how the work progressed.

Even the smallest villages in Italy all have electric light, whatever other features of modernity they may lack, but Deruta goes further than most. In the little place where we stopped to have our luncheon there was an image of the Madonna with an electric votive

lamp in front so arranged that it looked as though
Our Lady were warming her hands at it. While we
were waiting for our food to arrive, two small children came in, sate on the edge of chairs and eyed us
shyly. In a moment of foolish generosity, Harold gave
them each a penny. As a result we noticed a percepti-
ble increase in the price of our entertainment.

Between Deruta and Todi the Tiber occupies itself
mainly with making ox-bows and doing other contor-
tions in the valley. There is fat farming land on both
sides of the river and the people thereabouts seem to
have little to do with the stream, although at a number
of places we descried fishing apparatus tucked away
and left in all sorts of odd places. The heat was just as
intense as it had been all morning and the thing that
caused us our chief concern was the melting of the
cement that held the seams together and anxiety as to
whether we should be able to make Todi with the air
oozing out of our craft at various pores much faster
than we liked to contemplate. When we finally got to
the point just below Todi, and hauled the nearly deflated canoe ashore, we were glad enough to get a lift
up the long hill and into the town from an amiable
man with a car. It would have been a bad enough
tramp on an hot day without any loads to carry; to
have had to lug the canoe would have been almost

intolerable. It is all very well to start carrying thirty-five pounds up hill, but long before you get all the way up, the thirty-five pound burden seems to have increased to something like three hundred. The road from the river up to Todi, seated proudly on its hill-top, is both long and winding. The weight of the canoe, had we been obliged to carry it, would have completely damped our powers of admiration. As it was, we had a chance to enjoy the approach to the town, which is probably as wonderfully seated as any town in Italy.

X

TODI

====

A TOWN WITH TRIPLE WALLS

WARNINGS OF DANGERS TO COME

THE "STABAT MATER"

CHAPTER X

Todi

ARRIVED within Todi of the triple walls, our first concern was to get the canoe to a garage to have its melted seams re-cemented and vulcanised. As usual, the mere sight of the canoe was enough to cause a sensation and draw a crowd. When the proprietor of the garage put it down at one side of the street to examine the leaks, the street was immediately blocked by a throng of curious spectators and traffic came to a standstill. The canoe, therefore, had to be moved inside the repair shop for further inspection and mending.

The *canotto di gomma* in all its uncanny blackness and gumminess had been visible long enough, however, for its presence and its appearance, as well as its present purpose, to be bruited all over Todi within an incredibly short space of time. No doubt Dame Rumour was as busy and prolific with inventions and additions about us and our weird craft as she usually is. It would have been amusing if we could have heard some of the final versions of the story. At any rate, the reports were enough to set up a great excitement. Everybody knew that three *forestieri* had just come down the Tiber in a strange-looking black rubber thing that resembled a gigantic balloon tyre for an automobile, and that they intended to continue their journey in it to Rome. One and all they agreed that that way lay disaster and probably death. Our enterprise they regarded as sheer madness. The why you shall soon learn.

Meanwhile, having found an hotel, we separated. Geoffrey sate down to write, Harold wandered off to poke about and examine some architectural restoration that was going on, and Frank went off to sketch. When they met again they all had a story to tell. Geoffrey had been talking to or, rather, had been talked to by the hall-porter of the hotel, an obnoxious little creature who dogged his footsteps and kept asking him if he wasn't afraid. This conversation was carried on in French of a sort or, as Geoffrey put it, "I hung all the Italian I knew on a French peg, and he spoke Italian with a few French words thrown in here and there. However, to the porter's thinking, we were speaking excellent French." Harold and Frank together had come across a man who was connected in some way with the construction of roads in the district, and had been in America and therefore spoke

English. And Frank had been interviewed by the representative of a Roman newspaper, *La Tribuna*.

The sum total of their information was that there was a terrible danger ahead of us, something called *Il Forello*. At length we pieced the various stories together. *Il Forello* means a cleft or hole in the rock and, so far as we could gather, the Tiber at this point forced its way through a narrow passage where the mountain had been split asunder, in prehistoric times. This point lay about five miles below Todi. It appeared that in the middle of this passage the river went over a waterfall thirty feet high, and then continued through what was virtually an underground channel. In the old days they used to send timber through the *Forello* on its way to Rome, but the raftsmen had gone around the *Forello* by path and collected their rafts again at the other side. They would not go through with the timber, for, they said, after the falls it disappeared from view for about a hundred feet. The walls to this "canyon" were about a thousand feet high. No boat had ever been through, although attempts had repeatedly been made. They had all ended in disaster. The previous spring three men had set out to make the passage, but their endeavour had brought the usual misfortune. Their boat had been dashed to pieces on the rocks of the island that lies just before the falls; one man had been killed instantly, and the other two had just barely managed to swim to the shore and drag themselves out exhausted.

This, be it noted, was the description and story told us by the people of Todi, and it is fair to assume that the reader has formed much the same mental picture as we did at the time—the river gradually narrowing till you come to a cleft in the mountain; sheer walls towering above a turbulent stream about forty or fifty feet wide; a passage that never saw the sun; probably a narrow path running along the face of the cliff; a rocky island and, beyond it, a waterfall; and then a black tunnel through which the water boiled. Not a cheerful outlook, as you may imagine.

Before setting out on our expedition we had been told there were some bad rapids and whirlpools in the upper Tiber, but we had not been warned of any particular danger in the neighbourhood of Todi. We had come to Italy at that time on purpose to navigate the Tiber—a long-cherished design of Harold's—and, for the honour of old England and America, as well as for our own self-respect, we had no mind to abandon the project without at least having a go at this difficult place ahead of us. We were determined to send the canoe through *Il Forello* anyhow, and that one of us, at least, would go through with it if it were

The Porta Catena
at Todi

at all possible to do so. We were not going to be scared off by bogeys, and the only thing for us to do was to go and see for ourselves what the place was like.

The people of Todi, one and all, tried their best to dissuade us from going on with our mad design. They talked, they shouted, they gesticulated. One woman, learning that we really intended to go, despite all warnings, threw up her hands in a gesture of despair, shrugged her shoulders and departed.

When we went back to the garage to see how the repairs were progressing, and to order a car to take us down to the river early in the morning, we found more excitement and were informed that a New York car had just come into the garage and that the owner was anxious to see the three foolhardy Anglo-Saxons who were tempting Providence. We learned also another interesting piece of news, namely that a car was leaving Todi betimes the next morning to take a number of people to the mouth of *Il Forello* that they might have one last glimpse of us before we finally disappeared into the darkness. We were naturally rather amused and flattered.

Just across the street from his repair shop, the owner of the garage had a shop for all sorts of automobile accessories. After he had mended the leaks, he stood the canoe up on end in his shop window with the paddles crossed saltire-wise in front of it. He left the corrugated iron shutters of the shop rolled up all night and the electric lights on so that everybody in Todi might see the canoe. And everybody did. Also, we discovered, in the morning, that someone had written on the duckboard "Todi, 4 Settembre, 1929," and that the board was covered with names.

Todi is without question one of the most delightful hill towns of Italy, and yet it is almost unknown to travellers except by name and hearsay. The cause of this general neglect is doubtless the fact that it is remote, that it is not on the direct route by road between any of the better-known and generally visited places, and that it is not readily accessible by rail as the nearest railway station is about twenty miles away. Anyone who goes there will find more than ample compensation for the journey. There are plenty of "sights" of an high order, and the general atmosphere of the town, apart from the notable features of interest mentioned in the guide books, is reward enough in itself.

Todi is the ancient *Tuder* of Etruscan days, and from that time till well past the Middle Ages it was a stronghold and city of no little importance. Its natural position on top of a steep hill nearly a thousand feet

above the Tiber valley was apparently enough to recommend it strongly to the Umbro-Etruscans long years before the Roman domination spread over this region. The remains of the Umbro-Etruscan and Roman walls can be easily traced at numerous places within the city, and the mediaeval walls, which made the third ring of Todi's triple line of fortification, are still largely intact.

Todi has never lost its mediaeval aspect and you cannot walk its streets without feeling that you have completely left the outer world and stepped back four or five centuries. Everywhere are precious gems of mediaeval and Renaissance architecture in a setting that could not be more appropriate nor better suited to display their charms. As for the piazza, it is a bit of the most idyllic piazza composition your fancy could conceive. Somehow, directly you set foot within its charmed area, you instinctively feel that you are really taking part in a scene from *Pagliacci* or *Cavalleria Rusticana*. So dramatic is the quality of the piazza in every respect that it is hard to convince yourself that you are not in a trance and seeing something you had always dreamed about but never expected to behold with your waking eyes. You are tempted to pinch yourself to make quite certain you are not going to wake up and find the whole thing an illusion.

At the northeast corner of the piazza is the façade of the Duomo, rising above a platform approached by a flight of steps. The front of the cathedral is of the thirteenth century, but the building is much older than that and within you can see the thirteenth- and fourteenth-century work of the Comacine builders mingled with parts of the more ancient Romanesque structure. On the long south side of the piazza are the Palazzo del Popolo and, adjoining it, the Palazzo del Capitano. The Palazzo del Popolo, begun in 1213 and finished in 1228, now houses the Communal Museum and contains, besides the numerous Umbro-Etruscan fruits of excavation in the neighbourhood, a number of fine paintings, amongst them some of Lo Spagna's best work. The Palazzo del Capitano, built between 1290 and 1296, is a splendid Gothic structure in contrast with the more austere Romanesque manner of its neighbour, the Palazzo del Popolo. The stately outside staircases of these buildings, together with the steps leading up to the platform in front of the Duomo, add to the dramatic atmosphere of the piazza. At the other side of the piazza, facing east and at right angles with the Palazzo del Popolo and the Palazzo del Capitano, is the Palazzo dei Priori, built at the end of the thirteen century and partly rebuilt at the beginning of

*Street Scene
in Todi*

the sixteenth. The presence of the Duomo and these three communal palaces all fronting on the piazza, with all the other buildings architecturally consistent, makes it absolutely unique in its effect. Just beside the steps of the Duomo, a low parapet enables you to get an inspiring view far to the northward towards Perugia; to the south, at the end of an offset beside the Palazzo del Popolo, another parapet allows an equally lovely view of hills, valley and mountains.

Near or upon the site of the old Etruscan citadel, and not far from the castellated west gate, is the church of San Fortunato, begun in the thirteenth century but not completed till the beginning of the fifteenth—the façade, indeed, was never finished—which is probably one of the most perfect specimens of Italian Gothic architecture to be found. Here, under the high altar, is buried the mystic poet, Jacopone di Todi, the author of the *Stabat Mater*.

Notwithstanding the perfect and unspoiled mediaeval quality of Todi, there is no suggestion of gaunt ruin and decay. On the contrary, the place has an air of comfortable well-being and thrift and the whole city has the aspect of being just as well cared for and kept in repair as places like Florence and Perugia. This appearance of prosperity and tidiness is so marked and so universal that one could easily be deceived into believing the church of Santa Maria della Consolazione, just outside the walls, to be a structure of comparatively recent date instead of a building finished in the early part of the sixteenth century.

XI

"IL FORELLO, IL FORELLO!"

A BRIDGE AND AN AUDIENCE

FRENCH IN ITALY

GEOFFREY'S EXPERIENCE

RAPIDS AND WHIRLPOOLS

CHAPTER XI

"Il Forello, Il Forello!"

THE next morning we had breakfast at five
o'clock with a "Morituri vos salutamus" feeling
hanging over our heads, not knowing what the day of
our adventure might have in store for us—drowning,
shipwreck or what not. Sharp at six we left Todi and
the garage proprietor drove us in his car, with the
canoe on top, down to the Ponte Cuti where we were
to embark on the next stage of our river journey.

The Ponte Cuti is a mediaeval fortified bridge, a
splendid old stone structure on tall arches with a
strong tower guarding one end. Clustered nearby, as
though crowding close to the tower for protection, are
the houses of a small village. Despite the early hour
we had our interested audience consisting of most of
the villagers.

As we dropped downstream under the bridge we
looked up. There, ranged all along the parapet at the
side of the bridge were the two village *padres*, three
Franciscan friars who had suddenly sprung up out of
the earth, an old man with a pet sheep on a leash,
small boys, women, goats, dogs, and all the biped and

145

quadruped population of the place not otherwise
urgently engaged at the moment. The humans waved
farewell and gave us their blessing, and the animals
wagged their tails. Just below the bridge some women
were washing clothes on stones by the water side.
They, too, paused from their labours and wished us
godspeed. Everybody seemed genuinely concerned for
our safety.

It was a delightful morning, the forerunner of an
extremely hot day that brought great sunburn discomfort to Geoffrey's back and Harold's knees. We were
now getting somewhat away from the farming lands
and the banks of the river were more heavily and continuously wooded. The sun, just beginning his upward
course, was sending his rays aslant beneath the ilex
trees and poplars on our left and making shifting pat-
terns of light and shadow on the water around us. A
pleasanter scene of departure it would be hard to
imagine.

The river was growing broader and deeper in the
quiet reaches, and the rapids were also becoming more
and more frequent. Although the *Forello* was only
about five miles below Todi by road, by water it was a
good deal farther owing to the many bends of the
river. We were in feverish haste to get on and see what
the *Forello* was really like and whether we could get

through it as we hoped. The greater our impatience, the more resolved the canoe seemed to be not to move one iota faster than its ordinarily demure pace. To lighten our craft and expedite progress, Frank and Geoffrey frequently took turns afoot along the bank. Now that the mountains were drawing in closer and closer and cultivated fields were of rare occurrence, going along the bank was not easy. Both Frank and Geoffrey got their legs well scratched by brambles, and at one place the others did not see Geoffrey for over an hour while he went right over an hill, as there was no path by the river. At length he rejoined them by climbing down the rocky bed of a dried-up stream. For a while after that we all three remained in the canoe, although we often had to disembark for rapids that were too much blocked with boulders to shoot.

A little after nine at one of the rapids Frank and Harold were wading and Geoffrey was taking the canoe through, which meant that the canoe was taking itself through and Geoffrey, acting as anchor, was being dragged behind. Just as he had been let in for a complete ducking and his head was reappearing above water, he saw on the bank three men and a girl. One of the men addressed him in such fluent French that Geoffrey was sure he was French. As an actual fact, he and his three friends were all Italians and had never been out of Italy. It is a pity that such fluent French is not taught in our schools. They were the party that we had heard were setting out from Todi to see our attempt at the *Forello*.

They asked us to let them take photographs of us, and they insisted that we should come ashore and share their luncheon with them, although we had some of our own in the canoe. However, as we had breakfasted at five and had been having a very strenuous time since then, we were not averse to an half-past nine luncheon. We sate down in the shade of an ilex grove at the foot of the cliffs and did full justice to the cold chicken, ham sandwiches, peaches, grapes and wine. It was most kindly and courteous of these four strangers to take the genuine interest and concern they did, but such are the Italians. We shall always be grateful to our four friends Romolo Bondanini, Torquato Castellini, Milena Buglioni and Giuseppe Caprioli for the kindness and friendliness they shewed us that morning, even if they did believe —as we are certain they did—that the meal we were eating would surely be our last.

After our early luncheon we pushed on afoot to explore and after we had gone about three quarters of a mile, Harold and Frank decided to go back for the canoe. Geoffrey went on with the Italians but soon had to leave them as they had reached a place where it was impossible to go farther on foot except by crossing the stream. The next part of the story can be told only in Geoffrey's own words, as he alone experienced it: "We had come to the cleft in the mountain, but there was not the black hole we had expected. I said good-bye to our friends as they could not accompany me any farther.

"The dangerous part of the *Forello* was said to be a little more than half a mile farther on, for we had just passed the island. The walls of the mountain were sheer, jagged cliffs, with no vestige of the path we had expected to find, but owing to the lowness of the water a few rocks were shewing above the surface along the right bank. I swam across to them and walked as far as they went. Then I saw some more rocks farther down on the other side, so I swam to them. And so I went on, swimming backwards and forwards for about two miles.

"It was one of the most eerie experiences I have ever undergone. I was all alone and there was no sound except that of water rushing through rapids. Perhaps —who knew—the dreaded waterfall might be round the next bend ahead. Towering walls of jagged rock glowered above me, wide enough apart, however, to let in the welcome light of the sun. Each time I entered the water, with the roaring of the turbulent stream ahead, I wondered whether I would be swept away by some swift current and carried over the waterfall before I could save myself. I don't think I was frightened. I was just awed and indulging in the luxury of an entirely new experience of danger.

"At one point I thought that at last I had come to the notorious spot. The walls of the gorge were at their highest. I had walked as far as I could on the left bank, and fifty yards ahead of me a large pile of stones had been thrown up on the other bank. The water before me was deep, dark and ominous, and round the bend I could hear the raging of a troubled torrent. I entered the water with more trepidation than I had ever before known in my life. I swam across. Round the bend there was merely a more tempestuous rapid than usual, and when I had walked the length of the couple of hundred yards at my disposal I found the country was widening out again.

"As I had been gone an hour, I thought I had better go back for Harold and Frank. They could at least come as far as I had. I met them more than a mile back, Harold picking his course over the rocks at the end of the island, on his way to look for me, and Frank waiting in the canoe. I went on downstream again, traversing the distance much as I had before, while Harold and Frank navigated the canoe."

The passage of the rapids and whirlpools in the canoe made very nasty going for over half a mile, it must be admitted, and the voyage through the *Forello* was not a thing we should care to repeat very often. There was an unbroken succession of rapids and whirlpools, and some of the rapids it was impossible to take with anyone in the canoe owing to the presence of thickly-strewn boulders too near the surface for even the shallow draught of our rubber craft. At such places Harold and Frank had to wade gingerly through the water and rocks, holding on to the canoe, guiding it and occasionally lifting it, and then climb in as soon as the obstructions ceased, paddle across the whirlpool, and go straight into the next rapids. These they might have to take partly afoot, as before, or might be able to shoot sitting in the canoe. It was a tedious as well as a dangerous job and left no opportunity to enjoy the scenery, which was really very fine, as we eventually discovered when at last we had a chance to look back.

After we had run the last rapids and crossed the last whirlpool, Geoffrey got back into the canoe and we had a consultation under the welcome shadow of a great cliff, for the sun was now scorching. Frank was of the opinion we had passed the *Forello*. Harold was inclined to agree with him because the troublesome gorge we had just come through was where our Todi friends had told us the *Forello* was, and also where the ordnance survey maps indicated it. Geoffrey, however, said that even allowing for the imaginative nature of the Italians, where was the waterfall, and where was the tunnel that came after it? All the same, we were now in a broad and full-flowing stream, there were no more rapids in sight, and we decided to push on and see what happened.

From this point onward, we could really enjoy the scenery, looking backward, forward and to both sides. Back of us, above the gorge, rose the forest-covered mountain chain to a great height. Ahead of us were more mountains and forests, with rolling farm country extending right up to the lower foothills. At each side of us the country was gradually opening out and becoming more regularly cultivated. The water willows along the banks were much less in evidence than they had previously been, and the oaks and other trees on the shores were larger and cast a more generous shade.

When we had gone several miles we espied a farmhouse near the left bank. Harold insisted on stopping and going up to make enquiries so that we could definitely satisfy ourselves whether we had really come through the *Forello* or not. When Harold asked the farmer's wife where the *Forello* was, she answered that it was above and pointed to exactly the place we had just come from. "Then we're through it," said Harold. The good woman stared at us in amazement. Had we achieved the impossible? Had we come through the *Forello* in a boat? Yes, we had. We had been the first people, so they said, to navigate the *Forello*. Thereupon the farmer's wife and the farmer, and all their children and dogs came down to the river side to inspect the *canotto di gomma* which apparently astonished them as much as our recent exploit. They wished to feed us and shew us what humble hospitality they could, in true Italian fashion, but we still had some luncheon in the boat with us and we felt that we must push on, so we thanked them and took the will for the deed.

There can be only one explanation for all the dread story of the *Forello* and its impassable peril. You will have seen from the foregoing account that even at low water one cannot walk through the fissure in the mountain side. At high water in the spring when the snow-swelled floods come pouring down, there would not even be the stones that Geoffrey had used, and it is safe to assume that as no boat, according to all accounts, had previously been through the river at this point, it had, consequently, never been seen except from the mountain at a great distance above. At high water, looking down on a swift-running stream as it rushes over piles of stones such as we had encountered, and over projections in the walls, you get the impression from above that there is a distant drop, for the water would seem to be held up in places and then suddenly break loose. But nothing can explain the myth of the cavern through which the water is believed to run after the falls. This part of the story we had to conclude was pure invention.

One thing seems very certain. We could never have navigated the *Forello* if the river had been in flood. While there was a fair head of water, the conditions were far different from those that obtain in the spring, when the Apennine snows are melting, or even after a summer rain storm in the mountains when all the tributaries are pouring in their contributions and the river suddenly rises. We are also quite certain that we could not have traversed the *Forello* successfully in any other kind of craft than the inflated rubber canoe. Its structure was adapted for just such work. Being fashioned very much like an old Irish *curragh*, it could live in places where other boats would surely have come to grief. The rubber was resilient enough to withstand the buffetings and blows from boulders in the

rapids that we could not possibly avoid hitting; these
unavoidable obstacles would undoubtedly have
wrecked any stiffer boat in almost less time than it
takes to tell it. Furthermore, our canoe had no keel
and drew so little water that it gave us no serious
trouble in the whirlpools. We were occasionally spun
round two or three times, but without much difficulty
we managed to paddle off the revolving surface and
keep clear of the vortex.

We are not at all sure that we achieved anything
half so remarkable as people made out. The river conditions were altogether in our favour and our *canotto
di gomma* was peculiarly suited to just such occasions.
If, as they told us, we were the first to negotiate successfully this turbulent bit of the river, we can't help
thinking it incredible that in all these centuries no one
else had performed the same feat. At all events, the
Forello episode was somewhat of a lark and had its
lively spice of adventure. Perhaps we shouldn't have
enjoyed it as much if the people of Todi hadn't made
such a terrible bogey of the passage and told us it was
impossible. We were glad to be through safe and
sound with only bumps and a wetting. And we may
as well confess that we are glad to have the experience
behind us rather than to have it as something ahead of
us in the future. In this case we are quite content with

retrospect and we are ready to say, "Forsitan et haec olim meminisse juvabit."

The amusing thing about all the excitement over the *Forello* was that, after we had got safely through it, the worst was still to come, as you shall learn. The river was now much wider and the rapids, which occurred at fairly frequent intervals, were often more difficult. At some of them, although there was a great volume of water dashing along at a tremendous speed, there were so many big projecting boulders and so many snags and stakes that there was nothing for it but to plunge into the water ourselves, hang on to the canoe and lift it over the obstructions. In doing this, time and again we were nearly swept off our feet by the force of the current. When we came to rapids that were free of obstructions, as we did now and then, we felt truly jubilant at being able to shoot through with all three of us aboard. This was really fine sport.

The scenery was now much wilder than it had been before reaching Todi. There was considerably less cultivated land and, in many places, great tracts of forest came right down to the river. The mountains, too, seemed to be getting closer on all sides. Indeed, it looked as though the ridge directly ahead of us completely blocked our way. We knew that beyond was Orvieto crowning its vast rock, with the Paglia flowing at its foot, but all these things were still invisible. The only evidences of human habitation were a few distant walled villages and ruined castles on the mountain sides, silhouetted against the dark blue-green of the forests. As the afternoon advanced, nothing could exceed the beauty of the colouring and the play of light and shadow on the flanks of the encircling mountains, their jagged tops sharply outlined against an inexpressibly blue sky with faint dashes of amber to warn us of approaching sunset. With each bend of the river, a completely fresh panorama greeted our eyes. The contrasts of landscape were oftentimes startling in their abruptness.

About half-past four, on rounding a sharp bend of the river the scene totally changed. It had been wild and expansive; it now became intimate and pastoral. It had the mellow tenderness of a Corot or the soft mystery of one of the seventeenth century Italian *paesaggi*. The only thing needed to make the resemblance absolutely perfect was a Classic temple ruin on a lofty eminence above the stream. The surface of the water was as still as glass, with mirror-like reflections of the trees and rocks. On the left bank was a white-walled shepherd's cottage embowered in a grove of ancient oaks, the wooded hill rising close behind. On our right, venerable sycamores and ilex trees shaded the bank and cast their images in the still water; behind them were narrow strips of cornfields and vineyards. Before us, standing knee-deep in the stream beneath the shadow of a mighty rock, a herd of great fawn-coloured cattle with long branching horns recalled Classic memories of Europa or of ancient Mithraic rites. Near the shore a little water-snake scuttled away in afright. The whole scene was one of ineffable peace and calm. We were glad to ship our paddles and drift. Ahead of us, half way up the nearby hillside, were the village and castle of Corbara and we were debating whether it would be well to put up there for the night.

But the paradisial peacefulness was soon to be rudely shattered. Geoffrey was walking on the right bank, bemoaning his sunburn, and had wandered some distance inland trying to keep in the densest shade. He had espied rapids ahead and had shouted to the others to keep to the right bank, but they had not heard him. Suddenly he heard an ominous bump and saw a peasant in a blue shirt running towards the bank.

Geoffrey admits that his feelings were "I hope they've wrecked that blasted canoe for good and all." The sight that met his eyes was Harold standing on a rock, holding the canoe; Frank fishing for something in a pool between big rocks at the foot of a cliff; and,

immediately behind then, a boisterous young waterfall, about eight feet high, which he had sent them
over unwittingly—we hope. But, from his point of
view, the worst of it all was that the canoe had not
been damaged, although they had come slap down on
to a solid rock at the bottom of the fall, and Harold
had once more escaped with only the bottoms of his
shorts wet! "Whom the Gods love——!" The sole
damage had been that in trying to ward off a rock
Harold had broken the shaft of a paddle.

Not hearing Geoffrey's warning, Harold and Frank
had picked the least obstructed part of what appeared
to be merely rapids. Not till they were within twenty-
five feet of it did they discover they were headed for
a waterfall. It was too late then to do anything. It was
impossible to steer aside into a boulder and hold on to
it for the current was sweeping them onward at a
furious rate. What might be the proper etiquette for
canoeing over the edge of a waterfall they did not
know, and it wouldn't have done very much good if
they had, but in the natural course of things it seemed
best to take it head-first rather than sideways or backward, which would have been like trying to evade the
issue. As it turned out, head first seems to be the proper
way. This we note for the benefit of them that
may some time find themselves in a like predicament.

Under the circumstances, Harold and Frank did the only thing they could do—they steered straight on and, so to speak, "took the bull by the horns." The one really untoward incident of the episode was the large submerged boulder almost at the very edge of the falls. It was in trying to avoid this that Harold snapped the shaft of his paddle.

The descent from the edge to the bottom was instantaneous. Once at the bottom of the falls, the first thought that popped into the heads of the amazed canoeists was, "Now, the game's up. The canoe is surely done for!" To their utter astonishment, the *canotto di gomma* righted herself and came demurely to rest in a backwater between a couple of huge boulders, as though nothing unusual had happened. Incidentally, she had shipped surprisingly little water. It chanced to be a case of "All's well that ends well," but we cannot commend canoeing over waterfalls as a pleasant or comfortable business. Two of our party have done it once, perhaps you will say, with composure and nonchalance. They don't wish to try it again.

Having recovered the blade of our paddle from a pool into which it had floated, and having picked Geoffrey up from the right bank, we worried slowly along with our one whole paddle till we came to the ferry at Corbara, about three quarters of a mile down the river. As our propulsive force was badly crippled, and we didn't know how long it might take to repair the broken paddle, we thought we should now have to spend the night at Corbara whether we wished to or not. Hauling the canoe up on the bank at the ferry mooring, we started up the hill to find the village.

The ferryman's whitewashed cottage on the high river bank, the winding road past it, the over-arching sycamores and the whole character of the setting were strongly reminiscent of many a similar riverside scene in Pennsylvania or New York. Indeed, so far as appearances were concerned at this particular point, the Tiber might have been an American river.

Corbara, when we had toiled up the winding road and reached it, turned out to be but a tiny hamlet made up of a few of the humblest kind of houses. The castle was far above, along the same road. In the village, the local blacksmith was busy shoeing a yoke of oxen in a little open shed beside the road. It was interesting to see the great beasts swung into a cradle and lifted off the ground by turning a windlass. Then their legs were securely tied so that they could not kick, and the blacksmith was ready to begin nailing the iron plates to their hoofs in much the same way as he would shoe horses.

The carpenter, across the road from the blacksmith, undertook to mend our paddle. He made a splendid job of it and, when he had finished, the paddle was as good as new. When he had done he refused any pay and we had to contend with him and be very insistent to get him to take even a small sum for his time and labour. The kindliness and good will of these country folk are simply amazing, and they are always ready to do one a good turn. This friendly spirit you will find not only in remote country places like Corbara, but very generally throughout Italy. Is it any wonder that you cannot help loving the Italians?

The carpenter's wife kept a little wine and tobacco shop in the front of the house; her husband's workshop was at the back, up the side of the hill. While we were waiting for the paddle, we replenished our stock of cigarettes and had a brown jug of the local vintage. This refreshment was rather necessary for one member of the party as it was getting late and Harold always grows positively savage if he doesn't get his tea in the afternoon or, at least, something to drink in lieu of it.

It was in this little shop over our earthenware jug of wine that we reached a decision for the night. It was quite plain there was no place in Corbara where we could be put up. We should therefore have to push

on to Baschi, several miles below the junction of the
Paglia with the Tiber. Geoffrey was to set out immediately, cross the ferry and go cross country to Baschi,
which was only a short distance by land. There he
would arrange quarters for the night and then go
down to the river bank to await the arrival of the
canoe. Frank and Harold would start with the canoe,
as soon as the paddle was ready, and bring it around
to Baschi.

Accordingly Geoffrey set out straightway for
Baschi, having learned by heart the words *"Qual' è la
strada per Baschi?"* It was not long before we all discovered the folly of our plans, for it began to get dark.
Geoffrey wondered how the others would find him.
He was especially annoyed because he had only thirty
lire in his pocket and knew very little Italian beyond
"Qual' è la strada per Baschi?" On his way he met the
mailcart with its two Fascisti guards who stopped and
tried to talk to him. At last he took a little Latin and
all his Italian in one hand and said, *"Duo amici—
canotto di gomma—Tevere."* This seemed to work; in
any case, they went away grinning, and Geoffrey used
his new found knowledge on everyone he met. His
winning smile did the rest.

By the time he reached Baschi it was quite dark and,
what was more depressing, the Tiber lay a good three

or four hundred feet below. He found a steep, narrow path leading down, but even then he could get no nearer than forty or fifty feet above the water, so he could not see how the others were to land if they did arrive. At the end of an hour's waiting in pitch blackness, he concluded they couldn't be coming, so he climbed up again, got lost, and had to scale what was almost a cliff.

Meanwhile, Harold and Frank had left Corbara with the canoe and kept on down the river till it grew so dark that they could no longer see how to get through the rapids. Indeed, at one place, after taking what appeared to be an open channel they found themselves neatly caught in a wickerwork fish-trap, and a beautiful time they had getting out of it, too. Having extricated themselves from this embarrassment without any punctures, they concluded it was best to put the canoe in a safe place on the bank and go on a-foot to Baschi.

When they reached Baschi they learned that Geoffrey had been there. All the people knew about the coming of *Il Biondo,* as they called him, but they couldn't understand why this mad Englishman had gone down to sit on the bank of the river. Harold and Frank knew that Geoffrey was suffering terribly from sunburn and Harold's knees were painful from the

same cause. Finding it was possible to hire an automobile, they thought they would drive down to the
river, find Geoffrey and fetch him back. Just as the
car was coming into the piazza for them, the crowd
began to point and set up a shout, *"Ecco, Ecco! Il
Biondo viene!"* Sure enough, there was Geoffrey walking across the piazza, just back from his climb up the
cliff.

When we asked where we could get dinner and
lodging for the night, a jolly-faced man assured us
that it could all be arranged very easily if we would
follow him. So off we started to the other end of the
village under a convoy of the curious. We soon came
to a little *trattoria* of which our guide turned out to be
the proprietor. His wife, a stern and rather masculine-
looking woman, but kindly withal, when she bade us
good-evening punctiliously gave us the Fascist salute,
just like a man.

In due time our dinner was cooked, and very good
it was. The stern-faced Fascist *padrona* was a capable-
looking person, and she had proved herself a capable
cook. The jovial landlord, an ex-sailor as we discovered, sate with us and talked to us during dinner while
his wife and another woman waited on us. We were
really overwhelmed with attentions from the three
of them, and from the various children and friends

who kept coming in. When we were ready to go to bed, the landlord, his military-mannered wife and the other woman led the way with great circumstance and we were followed by a miscellaneous entourage. It was all very mediaeval. They seemed very loath to leave us. If we had let them, they would doubtless have undressed us and tucked us into bed themselves.

In the morning Frank went off and brought the canoe down to where the road from Baschi to Orvieto crosses the Tiber. Harold and Geoffrey, who were feeling much too brittle from sunburn to shew their wonted activity, walked down to meet him there. When at last the canoe came, there was still some sketching to be done in the village and Frank and Harold, therefore, climbed the hill again leaving Geoffrey to get his luncheon in a tiny vine-festooned *trattoria* at a bend of the road. Not the least non-plussed by Geoffrey's inability to order food in Italian, the *padrone* came to him with strands of uncooked spaghetti in one hand and a piece of salami sausage in the other to know whether they would do for lunch-eon, and managed the whole transaction by panto-mime. Thus one may eat in Italy, even though they cannot speak.

Baschi is a pleasant enough little hill town, but is absolutely devoid of anything notable to commend it

In the High Street
of Baschi

to the traveller. It consists chiefly of a single long street that widens out near one end into a piazza. At various intervals along this street are highly picturesque bits of composition that are thoroughly typical of Italian hill towns and pleasant incidents of the way if you are travelling by road, but there is no inducement sufficient to linger. Its chief charm lies in its setting and the view up and down the Tiber valley. At this point of our journey the logical place to stop would have been Orvieto, but thanks to the delay caused by our broken paddle Baschi was the nearest refuge.

Orvieto has been so often and so well described that it cannot be considered a little-known place, even by those who have not visited it. It is a curiously deceptive place from afar. Approached by the mountain road from the north, it looks low and you feel slightly disappointed when you have always been told of its lofty position. It is not till you get down to the valley, cross the Paglia just above its junction with the Tiber and then look up that you realise how high the city really stands and how tremendously strong was its position as a fortress from pre-Roman times till the Renaissance when the methods of warfare had completely changed. Your respect for Orvieto's loftiness will be vastly increased when you have climbed from the valley to the city gates. Your respect for the old Umbro-Etruscans who first fortified Orvieto will likewise go up a number of pegs.

Despite its great age—*Orvieto* was simply the *Urbs vetus* of the Romans—the city to-day wears an altogether mediaeval and Renaissance aspect. Everything is so solidly and so spaciously built that superposed modernism has produced little visible effect. And Orvieto can by no means be considered a dead city living chiefly on its past glories. It is a very wide-awake and prosperous place but, at the same time, it respects and cherishes its many monuments of antiquity. Orvieto's hotels are comfortable and, for anyone wishing to become thoroughly familiar with this part of the country either by motor or a-foot, no better place than Orvieto could be chosen as a base from which to radiate. The natural beauties of the country, its rich treasures of art and architecture, and its historical associations would fully repay any length of sojourn one might feel inclined to make. Orvieto and the surrounding neighbourhood for many miles deserve to be far better known than they are.

XII

FROM THE PAGLIA TO THE NERA

———————————————————

MEDIAEVAL ITALY

MORE RAPIDS

EARLY ROMAN WORK

CATHEDRAL AND CITADEL

CHAPTER XII

From the Paglia to the Nera

THE course of the Tiber seems to be divided naturally into a series of distinct periods or episodes, and the changes from one episode to another occur with little transition but much dramatic abruptness.

From the source high up on Monte Fumaiolo to Perugia, the river may be said to be passing through the stages of its infancy and irresponsible youth. From its emergence into the Umbrian plain at Perugia onward to Todi, its more or less placid course may be likened to a tranquil period of early maturity. From Todi to the junction with the Paglia, just below Orvieto, there is a solitary and tempestuous career with alternating incidents of passionate violence and stately composure when the stream seems to be fighting out its destiny and rounding out its forceful character. Thence to Orte, or its junction with the Nera just below, though its impetuous ardour is unabated, it seems to have gained a steadier balance and to be more approachable and patient of the advances of puny humankind. From Orte to the sea it gradually leaves the companionship of the mountains and, without losing any of its determined vigour, as it traverses the Campagna it puts on a certain leonine sobriety which it preserves unbroken to Ostia.

From Todi to Orvieto the Tiber forces his way by the most direct route through a knot of the Apennines. No railway traverses this lonely and intractable though not uninhabited region, and there is no direct main road. Owing to the configuration of the land and the mountain barriers, the highway from Orvieto to Todi follows a much longer and circuitous course. This intervening region is dotted with tiny villages and hamlets in the remote folds of the hills, but they can be reached only by steep, tortuous and difficult by-ways. Occasionally these trails—for some of them are little better than that—come down to the river where there is a clumsy barge ferry worked by cables or chains stretched from bank to bank. There was such a ferry at the farm where we stopped to find out whether we had really passed the *Forello* or not. If you wish to penetrate into truly mediaeval Italy, preserved intact with very little change for centuries, here is the place to explore. As a means of access, we could suggest going either a-foot or on horseback and starting from Todi or Orvieto. Another way would be to use the river as a mode of approach and means of communication, if you arrange to launch a canoe below the *Forello*; we should certainly not recommend a passage of the *Forello* under ordinary circumstances for anyone on an holiday or pleasure bent. On such an expedition you are certain to reap a rich harvest of highly original and interesting experience. The beauty of the scenery, too, is of the first order.

At the junction with the Paglia the river meets the main line of the railway from Florence to Rome, and thence onward river and railway keep close company all the way to the sea. The Paglia rises on the side of Monte Amiata, an high volcanic mountain to the northwest of Orvieto. In summer the volume of water it brings to the Tiber is inconsiderable, but a glance at its broad stony bed is enough to shew what a mighty contribution it adds in the winter and spring, or after mountain storms, even had you no personal acquaintance with it at such times.

From Orvieto and Baschi, though the recommended highways dodge back and forth in the mountains, now leaving the river, now approaching it again, it is always possible to get one of the by-roads coming down to the valley to the railway stations, most of which are at a distance from the towns which they serve and whose names they bear. In many cases the stations are two or three miles away from the towns

and are reached by a diligence or omnibus at train
times, as at Baschi. It is easy, therefore, to do as much
or as little of this part of the river by canoe as you wish.

The river itself presents a series of still-flowing
reaches, broken by rapids and shoals, in much the same
way as higher up. There is a greater and gradually increasing volume of water, however, and some of the
rapids are apt to give you a very lively time getting
through them. The shoals and rapids usually occur
where the current zig-zags across the stream from
bank to bank and are caused through the piling up of
boulders and shingle by the force of the water in the
winter and spring floods. When some of these ac-
cumulations of boulders and shingle get mixed up
with uprooted tree trunks and snags, they form barriers not unlike in appearance to the beaver dams you
encounter on the rivers of upper Canada. Canoeing on
this part of the Tiber, indeed, offers a number of
parallels to Canadian canoeing. For much of the way
the valley is narrow with the mountain slopes coming
close to the river and affording many intriguing views
of walled villages and castles perched aloft. In point
of walled villages and castles there is no resemblance
to Canada, of course; in such incidents the Tiber is
unique.

Not far beyond Castiglione in Teverina is Atti-

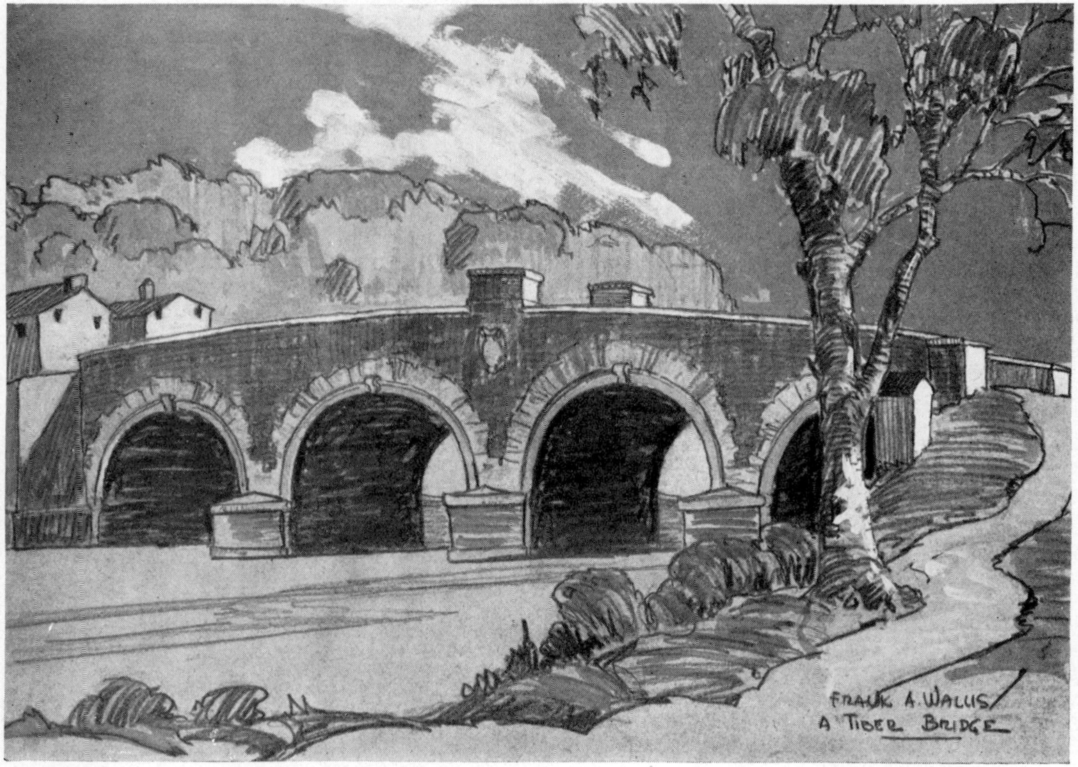

A Tiber Bridge
below Orvieto

gliano lying on a flat at the foot of the mountains with a fascinating old castle nearby. Directly across the river, on its right bank, bold wooded headlands jut out above the stream. Past Giove the land undulates on the left while it is rugged and beetling on the right bank. Mugnano, perched like Baschi on the steep hillside, greets the eye a little to the south. Not far to the west of Mugnano is Bomarzo on its steep, rocky eminence, distinguished by its picturesque setting and its Etruscan remains. Still farther south you see the heights of Bassano where the Romans won great victories over the Etruscans three centuries before the Christian era. Thence the distance to Orte is not great.

Orte is known chiefly as the railway junction between the main line from Rome to Florence and the branch line that goes northeastward to Foligno and Perugia. Furthermore, if anything happens to the trains in the way of an hot box or other cause of delay, it is always at Orte that the mischance occurs. As so often happens in the mountain regions of Italy, the station and the town are far apart. Orte town is two miles north of Orte station, and is one of the most unvisited places in all Italy. Baron Baedeker, beyond noting that there is a good railway restaurant at the station, dismisses the place with the bare statement that it was the ancient Horta of the Romans and that

it "presents no object of interest beyond its situation."
It might be an interesting diversion, and also profit-
able, some time to set out on a tour to all the places in
Italy that Baron Baedeker "praises with faint damns."
On such an expedition you would certainly find many
things worth while, to say nothing of frequent picturesque satisfactions.

Orte is built on a precipitous rock overhanging the
Tiber and many of its houses are in great part of early
Roman construction. There is a pleasant little piazza
and the narrow streets, which run to the edges of the
lofty rock on which the town is built, yield fascinating
vistas of distant countryside and mountain enframed
by archways and tunnels. The town is clean and well
kept, and the habit of putting out from the windows
pots of blooming plants gives it a cheery aspect. At the
extreme end of the town, on a separate crag, are a few
remaining ruins of a mediaeval castle. The only possible access to this fortress was by a narrow bridge
carried on tall arches across the ravine, the last span
crossed by a draw which has long since disappeared.
Without nosing into such towns as Orte, it is impossible to have any true conception of the character of the
Tiber valley or of the country enclosing it.

Two miles lower down and just about opposite the
railway station, the Nera debouches from its rocky

gorge and pours into the Tiber a volume of water equal to or greater than its own before the junction. The Nera, indeed, is the Tiber's greatest and most important tributary, anent which the Romans have a saying:

Il Tevere non sarebbe il Tevere
Se la Nera non gli desse da bevere.

The valley of the Nera, especially the deep gorge by Narni, affords river scenery that cannot be surpassed for wild and rugged beauty.

Orte is regarded as the head of navigation on the Tiber. Below that point there are no rapids to present difficulties, although the current is both swift and strong. Above Orte the navigation is confined to rafts of timber that come down in the autumn, winter and spring. At one time small steamers went up the river as far as Ponte Felice, about fifty-one miles above Rome, while large barges were towed as far as Orte, which is some seventy miles above Rome by the winding course of the river. More recently, owing to the formation of bars and obstructions higher up, the steamers went only as far as Scorano and the barges to Ponte Felice.

In ancient times the river seems to have been utilised to a far greater extent than in more modern days.

Livy puts into the mouth of Camillus a speech in which he refers to the Tiber as a stream on which corn could be floated down to Rome from the interior and the produce of other nations brought up from the sea. According to Pliny the Younger, in winter and spring boats went down the Tiber from Città di Castello to Rome bearing the produce of the upper valley, and there are other allusions in Classic times to more or less traffic borne on the waters of the river above Rome. To-day river traffic above Rome is all but non-existent. Since the Renaissance, various schemes have been advanced for rendering the Tiber navigable, of which the most feasible seems to be the construction of a canal practically parallel with the river and fed by it. Above Orte the stream is far too temperamental and subject to sudden fits of violence to place much dependence upon any programme of deepening.

Although the final stage of Father Tiber's course may really be said to begin at his marriage with the Nera, so far as his banks are concerned, their mountainous character continues some distance farther to the south until we reach the edge of the Campagna. Before reaching the Campagna, the valley at different points broadens out to a considerable width and gives plenty of room for well cultivated farm land on both sides of the river. Roads come down from the hills and cross the plain at frequent intervals and it is now always easy to leave the river and strike off into the hills to explore the towns, distant views of which whet curiosity and stimulate imagination.

Of these towns one of the most inviting is Civita Castellana. Whether the greatest charm of Civita Castellana lies in the town itself and the treasures it contains or whether it is the perennially delightful view of Soracte with its saddle and twin peaks, we have never been quite able to decide. The town is full of a fascinatingly elusive quality that produces a very curious effect. All the time that you are there you feel that the place somehow has a great deal more up its sleeve than it reveals, and this strange sensation does not grow less with repeated visits. Civita Castellana's chief gem, of course, is its mediaeval Cathedral with a thirteenth century porch adorned with rich Cosmatic work. Although the interior was a good deal messed up early in the eighteenth century, much that is very fine remains intact and the crypt especially is deserving of a visit. Besides the Cathedral, there is the Citadel, designed by Sangallo the Elder, and there are old Etruscan walls and Etruscan tombs in the deep ravines that surround the town; nearby, likewise, are remains of Etruscan temples. All these, to be sure, are "sights" that any well trained *cicerone* of the place

would unfailingly take you to see. But not a little of
the fascination inheres in the trifling things a native
cicerone would not think worth noticing or mention-
ing—a fountain here, a bit of old wrought iron there,
a crumbling arch, the remnant of a mediaeval house-
front, or a shop where they sell cheap native pottery
and copperware along with all manner of strange odds
and ends to be found nowhere else but amongst the
merchandise of an Italian hill town general emporium.
It would be hard to find a place where the obsession
to nose about takes stronger hold upon you. And then
there is the natural setting, with the eerie ravines full
of ancient Etruscan memories and frowning rocks
that Horace Walpole and his Romanticist contemporaries would have described as "horrid"; there is the
wide outlook over the Tiber valley below; and always
there is Soracte cleaving the sky with a jagged line
that is just as unmistakable amongst the Italian peaks
as are the Wittenham Clumps in Berkshire.

If you are minded to climb Soracte, you can best
do so by going to the village of Sant' Oreste whence a
trail leads up to the monastery of San Silvestro. The
view from the top is one of the most admirable you
will get anywhere in Italy and well worth the labour
of the ascent. Incidentally, it will greatly clarify your
notions of central Italian geography. No wonder the

Old Chapel
Nazzano

old Romans built a temple to Apollo on this noble height.

Nearly all the walled towns and ancient sites visible from this part of the Tiber valley are worth visiting, but one place especially, Nazzano, will always keep a warm spot in our memory. Just below Filacciano, on the right or west bank, there is a great hook of the highlands extending into and almost shutting off the valley. High up the mountain side, in the corner of this hook and looking towards the south and east, is Nazzano, the windings of the Tiber below you spread out for miles to the south, while to the east and south beyond the river your eye wanders over the Sabina, that mysterious hill country where few travellers ever penetrate and where untold treasures still await archaeological investigation.

The town contains nothing of particular note that would be starred in a guide-book, but the whole *ensemble* is so subtly captivating that you feel amply compensated for the trouble of getting there. The kindliness of the people, too, wins your heart. We arrived there at luncheon time, and with minds intent on food. There was no inn and the prospect of a meal was not promising. We asked at a poor little shop— the only place that offered the faintest hope—if we could get some bread and sausage or, failing that,

some cakes of chocolate. The little old woman who
presided over the place suggested that we might like
some luncheon, a suggestion we eagerly grasped at.
In ten minutes she had got us up as good a luncheon
as one could wish, deliciously cooked, and spread in
an immaculate little back parlour paved with brick
and curtained with chequered yellow material that
would have excited the envy of a swank interior
decorator.

XIII

THE CAMPAGNA

A GREY-BROWN DESERT

THE VILLAS OF ROMAN DAYS

ZENOBIA

LANDING AT ROME

CHAPTER XIII

The Campagna

JUST about Castelnuovo di Porto you emerge so gradually into the Campagna that you are scarcely aware of any marked change in the face of the land. Indeed, from the river, the change is less noticeable than it would be from the road because in a canoe you are so much lower than the top of the banks that your near field of vision is blotted out and you can see only the more distant objects unless you go ashore for a survey.

The Campagna, in the minds of most people, is an ill-defined area. Ninety-nine out of an hundred would be hard put to it to say just where the Campagna begins and where it ends. Furthermore, a great many people have a general impression that the Campagna is a flat plain. As a matter of actual fact, it is anything but flat. While there are certain comparatively flat areas within its limits, the greater part of the surface of the Campagna is undulating, with a succession of long swelling elevations and depressions like the troughs and crests of the sea after a storm.

Properly speaking, the Campagna is that great undulating plain surrounding Rome, approximately forty miles long by thirty miles wide. It is bounded to the north and northeast by the old Ciminian belt of craters around Viterbo and by the Sabine hills to the east of the Tiber; to the east it is shut in by the Sabine hills and the fore-Apennines; to the south it is enclosed by the Alban hills; and on the west it is terminated by the coast.

The general impression conveyed by the Campagna to-day is one of utter desolation and barrenness. Approaching by road, as you descend the last hills from the north, you feel that the Eternal City is sitting in the midst of a grey-brown desert. There is little evidence of either human habitation or cultivation—nothing but an austere waste, extending from the city to the distant hills, the monotony relieved only by an half-ruinous farmstead here, a few arches of broken aqueduct there, or a couple of lonely stone pines. The entrance from this quarter is undeniably disappointing, and tolerable only in the late afternoon when the lengthening shadows and mellow light soften the air of stark dreariness.

If you enter Rome by rail, the approach is no less depressing, especially if you come from the direction of Civita Vecchia. After such an entrance through the grim, furrowed, sun-baked and dust-covered Campagna, it takes a stranger about three days to recover from the sense of disappointment before he can begin to feel and appreciate the charm of Rome. Nor will he get much relief if, during those first few days of shattered ideals, he makes an expedition by steam tram to Hadrian's Villa and Tivoli. After passing the Basilica of San Lorenzo, the whole way thither seems an unmitigated stretch of weary, sun-bleached desolation. Even in the freshness of winter or early spring, there is little to allay the utter tedium and monotony.

Of all the possible ways of coming into Rome, approach by the Tiber would least shock the expectations of anyone who had never been there before. From the river you see less of the negative environment and your eyes rest chiefly on the lines of the blue hills all round the horizon. Then, too, there is the refreshing greenery of the banks and of the trees growing here and there along the course of the stream. As you come near the city you see ahead of you the wooded slopes of Monte Mario with the Villa Madama standing boldly out from its green background, to the left the rounded tree-clad eminence of Monte Parioli, and before long you glide under the time-mellowed arches of the Ponte Milvio. After that, you soon find yourself passing between the high stone-faced and parapeted embankments that line both sides of the Tiber on its

way through the city. Then comes the landing at the
steps of the Ponte Margherita. You are in Rome without being hurt by the ancient scars of the surrounding
country.

Notwithstanding the generally dreary aspect of the
Campagna, so shocking or, at least, so unalluring to
the stranger, those of us who know and love Rome
have a genuine affection for the Campagna also—an
affection bred, perhaps, of the long acquaintance
needed to recognise its merits as well as its shortcomings. Be that as it may, the Campagna possesses a
potent spell to which, sooner or later, you are sure to
succumb. Harold always stoutly maintains that, to
him, the Campagna seems to belong not so much to
Rome as it does to the old Etruscans and the pre-
Roman world. He insists that over it broods an air of
ancient Etruscan mystery, and he would not be in the
least surprised to encounter either sibyls or satyrs en-
sconced behind some lonely knoll, or sheltered in one
of those round wattled shepherd's huts, built exactly
as they were built two thousand years ago and more.

Geoffrey and Frank pooh-pooh this eerie sensibility
of Harold's. They say if there is anything brooding
over the Campagna it is either dust clouds or malaria.
They are perfectly willing to let Harold consort with
sibyls and satyrs, if he likes, or with the ghosts of long-

departed Etruscan worthies but, for their part, they have no stomach for such folk. However, Geoffrey and Frank haven't known the Campagna as long as Harold has, they are not as much steeped in Roman archaeology, and they have little regard for his touch of Scottish second-sight, sensibility to psychic influences or whatever it may be. They are quite convinced that the satyrs of old were nothing but ordinary, everyday cowherds or goatherds with goatskin breeches, hairy side out, much like their successors of the present day—considering the conservatism of the Italian peasant, not an altogether unreasonable supposition.

Those who look at the Campagna as it is to-day, and see in it only an oppressive area of vast loneliness and desolation, find it hard to realise that it was once both populous and prosperous and that its surface was covered with farms, villages, lordly villas and temples. In short, under the Empire, it was like a great continuous park. Along the banks of the Tiber were everywhere abundant evidences of man's successful efforts at embellishment. Despite any difficulties that confronted them, the Romans had made the shores into eligible sites for country houses. Pliny the Elder says that "all the rivers in the world together were not peopled, nor adorned with such a multitude of villas as the single river Tiber." Claudian, centuries later, having in mind the goodly houses and the splendidly adorned villas between which the Tiber flowed, prophesies the time when "the Rhine shall be lined, after the fashion of the Tiber, with mansions pleasing to the eye."

To-day all traces of these erstwhile glories of the golden age are vanished. Where once were groves and fruitful gardens with ample orchards, wherein did grow all manner of fruits, are now only treeless wastes. Where once were towns and villages, not a trace of human abodes now remains. Where once were mighty temples of the gods, we now see only a solitary peasant tending a few scattered sheep or goats. Barring the occasional farmsteads already mentioned, half-ruinous or altogether deserted, almost the only houses you will find are the remains of seventeenth century villas, built when there was for a few years an attempt to revive the Campagna's former prestige as a place of rural abode. The countryside seems as completely forsaken as the tombs along the ancient highways. If you seek the only remaining tangible evidence of this quondam prosperity, you must dig in the grass-grown mounds that have formed over the sites where buildings stood. Hadrian's Villa is an outstanding example of what such digging would reveal.

How the Campagna was reduced to its present state is a long, long story and too well known to need rehearsal here. What it once was, it might become again. Under the present intelligent programme of reclamation and restoration, at which a good beginning has already been made, some of us may yet see the Campagna well advanced on its way towards rehabilitation in a manner befitting the City it surrounds.

The visitor to Rome who fails to visualise in some measure the condition of the Campagna in the heyday of its prosperity, and thinks of it only as a treeless and mostly untilled waste, can never fully appreciate Rome herself nor the part the Campagna played in the life of the city. Let us try to picture briefly this mountain-girdled plain in the days when the Romans looked upon it as a desirable place for suburban or rural dwelling, when its irrigation was carefully provided for, and when it was green with groves, orchards and the gardens of villas.

As Lanciani has pointed out again and again—and other archaeologists have done the same—Rome was not cut off in ancient times by a stretch of dreary desert from her lesser neighbours such as Veii, Nomentum, Tibur, Praeneste and Tusculum. Vineyards, farms, olive orchards and the well-treed gardens of villas formed an almost unbroken area of park that might compare favourably in beauty and well-kept aspect

with many a rural neighbourhood in England. In one
part of the Campagna, indeed, could be counted as
many as ten patrician villas within a square mile. In
the light of indubitable records, we can confidently
picture the Campagna as presenting an aspect of beau-
tified cultivation not unlike the glorious belt of villas
encircling Florence to-day. From the contemporary
descriptions of these villas in the Campagna, many of
whose sites are now certainly identified, we know how
splendid was their architecture, how rich were their
decorations, how luxurious their appointments, and
how delectable their gardens. It was only towards the
Maremma that the Campagna was left well nigh un-
touched by man and not held a desirable place of resi-
dence. There the land was covered with forests full
of game. Through this region Pliny the Younger frequently passed on his way to his seaside villa at Laurentum. Of this land he says:—"The aspect of the
country is not monotonous, because the road sometimes runs through ancient forests, sometimes through
meadows and pasture land where grow and prosper
herds of horses and oxen, and flocks of sheep, which,
driven from the mountains by the early frosts, come to
winter in the tepid Campagna."

How different is all this from what we see to-day,
and yet how possible of realisation once again! It is

not fair to modern Rome if we fail to envision this
great past of the Campagna. Then, too, there are the
boundless rich associations of the Campagna's story.
Think of the sulphur springs and the present bath-
houses on the way to Tivoli, and then think of the
baths Agrippa built nearby with "colonnades of verde
antico, marble and mosaic floors, basons of gilt bronze
or precious marble, statues, busts, gardens, fountains
. . . the whole group surrounded and shaded by the
wood sacred to the health-restoring nymphs." Think
of the goodly company of ancient Romans—Romans
whose names are household words throughout the
civilised world—who lived in neighbouring country
places on the Campagna, entertained one another in
their houses, and held almost daily domestic converse
in the intimate management of their estates!
Think of the group of eminent lawyers who lived near
each other by the slopes of the Alban Hills and constantly hobnobbed with each other in their gardens or
porticoes over the legal questions of the day! Think of
Zenobia sent by Aurelian to spend the remainder of
her captive life in a beautiful villa near to Hadrian's
Villa, just below Tivoli, where she lived in privacy
and comparative freedom in the manner of a Roman
matron! The Campagna is full of memories such as
these, and countless more besides.

And with all this glory of the Campagna, the Tiber was not ignored. At one time it was the vehicle by which were borne to Rome her foreign supplies of corn and all the rich merchandise of tributary lands. The luxuries of the Orient came up the Tiber and were landed at the docks of Rome. The precious marbles to adorn her palaces and villas and her temples and public buildings came up the Tiber and were unloaded at the dock called Marmoratum. Though many of the larger sea-going ships were unladen at Ostia and their cargoes transferred to craft of shallower draught, the commerce carried by the Tiber in the days of Republican and Imperial Rome totalled a tremendous volume.

The potential value of the Tiber to-day as a means of transportation has not been overlooked. The river itself is too temperamental, too subject to sudden floods, and too violent in its outbreaks, to allow of satisfactory navigation very far above Rome. The strong and swift current is also a further obstacle, and the vast amount of solid deposit brought down by the river would always be an obstacle. But with the construction of a canal fed by the river, water transportation might be extended far up the Tiber valley. And there is no limit to what Italian engineering and the present wise policy of government works might accomplish. The volume of water descending the Tiber is amply sufficient; in summer the volume of water discharged by the river is as great as that discharged by the Thames and Severn together; in winter it is much greater.

If the Campagna to-day is full of memories but without many visible reminders of its ancient greatness, the towns on the slopes surrounding the Campagna and within easy distance of Rome afford plenty of interest to one who treads their little visited streets. There is Palestrina—the ancient Praeneste—for one, with its marvellous mosaics, and there is Palombara-Sabina, for another, with its fifteenth century castle and its ninth century abbey church of San Giovanni. To name only two more of the towns within ready reach of Rome, there is Nomentana, the ancient Nomentum, and there is Monte Rotondo, which occupies the top of one of those characteristic conical hills at the edge of the Campagna and intrigues the curiosity of everyone going to Tivoli.

The last night of our voyage down the Tiber we spent at Monte Rotondo. It was the only place on our whole journey where our quarters were not scrupulously clean. In fact, they were quite unpleasant though apparently the best the town afforded, and we were glad to be out of them. This condition, it should be added, is quite exceptional in Italy. It has always been our experience that, go where you will, even in the humblest places, you can almost invariably count on finding clean and comfortable beds and clean rooms.

Notwithstanding the unsatisfactory lodgings at Monte Rotondo, we could not be blinded to the fact that the place is full of picturesque attraction, so much so that we had a hard time during the late afternoon in keeping track of Frank who was always wandering off to sketch and getting lost. The subjects, however, were well worthy of all the attention they got and all the hunting parties they caused. The piazza of Monte Rotondo, graced by its Renaissance fountain, is full of the pulsing life of this little town and an entertaining place to linger in. From the ends of all the streets there are widespread views of the Campagna with the dome of Saint Peter's rising in the distance.

Bright and early in the morning we were down at the river—several miles from the high-lying town—for the last lap of our water pilgrimage to Rome, anxious to arrive at our destination and get cleaned up but sorry that our unconventional and highly momentous journey was nearing its end. The mists were still rising in wreaths from the water and its surface was like a mirror. A swift current favoured us, but despite that and our strenuous paddling our flat-bottomed, keel-

In the Streets of
Monte Rotondo

less craft seemed reluctant to move fast enough to suit us. With the willows and the reeds along the banks rising high above our heads, and confined as we were in the restricted oval of our canoe, we felt like Moses in the bullrushes waiting to be discovered.

We *were* discovered, soon after passing under the Ponte Milvio, not by Pharaoh's daughter but by an eight-oared shell full of young Romans out for early morning exercise. Our appearance completely upset their stroke and turned them speechless. They had never before seen anything like our *canotto di gomma*, and to say they were utterly flabbergasted is putting it mildly. They stared at us with eyes and mouths wide open, and they could not have been more thoroughly amazed if we had suddenly dropped from Mars in front of them. Our personal aspect probably astonished them no less than what looked to them like a black India rubber cushion in which we were calmly proceeding downstream.

Recovering some measure of composure and their manners at the same time, and having decided we were fellow human beings after all, they spoke. Misled by Geoffrey's leonine shock of fair hair, which was very much in evidence, and likewise by his ten days' growth of flavous facial fur, they thought we were *Tedeschi* and addressed us in German. That didn't answer at all as none of us understood a word of German, so Harold answered them in Italian and told them whence we had come and where we were going. Incidentally, he had to add a few words of explanation about our boat. Four more shells full of Roman oarsmen whom we met soon afterwards we demoralised as thoroughly as we had the first.

Our friends in Rome had expected us to arrive on this particular morning and had intended coming down to the river to meet us. They had not imagined, however, that we would come so early. Frank and Geoffrey, in hopes of a brass band or some equally blatant kind of publicity to celebrate the accomplishment of our journey, were all for killing time till an hour when our friends were likely to come down to the Ponte Margherita to greet us. Harold, with his usual obstinacy, insisted on pushing on. It was Saturday morning and he was determined, willy-nilly, to get to the hotel, have a bath and shave, and reach Barclay's Bank in time to get his mail before early closing. It was all very well to get the mail, but Frank and Geoffrey were convinced that Harold's real cause of haste was, first, his dislike of what they considered legitimate attention and, second, his unreasonable desire to shave. It had been a day and a half since he had been shaved and he was getting restive. He was always delaying things by hunting up a barber and being shaved with a foolish insistence on *feeling* respectable. His excuse was that the prickliness of a growing beard made him uncomfortable. It also made him savage—just as much so as not having his tea in the afternoon. Despite the entreaties of Frank and Geoffrey, he never would let the fur grow on his face and look the part.

So, then, we landed at the Ponte Margherita steps without any more sensation than the appearance of our *canotto di gomma* ordinarily occasioned. Being at the bottom of the embankment, and therefore out of sight of most of the passers-by, we had but a small audience as we "de-blew" the canoe and rolled it up so as to be able to stow it on top of a taxi. With Harold chuckling over our quiet entrance into Rome, we climbed the steps, piled into a taxi, collected our bags and made for the Palazzo Hotel where we effected a transformation to reappear "clothed and in our right minds."

But the Tiber trip had not yet reached its final stage. Our arrival had been seen by too many people for it to pass unnoticed. Rumour travels with more than electric rapidity in Rome. That night at dinner on the terrace of the Castello de' Cesari our friends divulged the fact that the newspapers had got hold of the story of a strange floating contrivance that had come down the river in the early morning with three *forestieri* in it and that our pictures were to be taken with the canoe the next morning at the Ponte Margherita.

At the appointed time, therefore, we turned up in our canoeing clothes, got into the canoe, paddled about and duly posed for the photographic performance—all this with much interested attention from the occupants of the boat houses and house-boats who shewed no end of curiosity about every particular of the craft that had brought us safely through the *Forello* and refused to be vanquished by the falls of Corbara in spite of Geoffrey's malevolent hopes.

Our canoe trip Down the Tiber and Up to Rome is now only a memory. But it will ever be a lively and cherished memory of days well spent, of wholesome excitement, and of honest weariness at each day's end; a memory of friendly and amiable people at every stage of our journey, and of warm hospitality in the towns and villages where we stopped; a pleasant memory of seeing one of the loveliest parts of Italy in a totally fresh and peculiarly satisfying way; a memory of close acquaintance with a noble river our respect for which has deepened into genuine affection.

We can wish no better fortune to travellers in Italy than that they may traverse the same region we did under auspices as pleasant. Whether they elect to follow the river, as we did, or whether they prefer to approximate our route by road, they will find in the country we covered bountiful compensations for any inconveniences incident to journeying altogether off the beaten track.

INDEX